Welcome to the World of Podcast Production! This book is aimed at both complete beginners and also existing podcasters who want to move to the next level and to attract further listeners to their podcast episodes.

The entire production of a podcast can be divided into three main elements:

Editorial, Technical and Promotion.

Editorial
Technical
Promotion

-**Editorial.** This is concerning mostly the actual content that you want to include, the features, the structure of each episode, the guests you'd like to interview.

- **Technical.** How you're going to record, edit and mix your podcasts. There's a big choice here with various choices for people who love to do things themselves with high end software or use a web-based service who can make things easier for you, but you lose a bit of detailed control.

I'll show you the hardware solutions you may wish to consider if you and your guests are going to record physically in one place each episode.

- **Promotion.** This is how you tell the world you're there, and I'll have a wide range of options for you on top of the must-do things a podcast should do to get found on the top directories.

I also completely understand that you may be one of many types of people who want to produce podcasts. For example, you may be an existing voice over artist with their own studio, looking to narrate and produce podcasts for your clients.

You may be a hobbyist with an absolute passion for a subject that you would love to make regular podcasts on for people who have similar interests around the globe. You may be a marketing person in an organisation, who has realised that traditional means of marketing just isn't working anymore, and you want to take advantage of the power of the podcast!

Maybe you're an expert, or an agent or representative of an expert, who wants to see what all this podcast fuss is about, and to discover that you could get exposure for yourself or your clients easily to a highly targeted audience by being interviewed or featured on a wide range of much listened to podcasts!

You could even be a manufacturer of a product, or someone who offers a service to a small, specialised niche of people, where being involved with an existing podcast, or creating your own, would really hone in on a group of eager customers for you!

Or you could be someone who works for a broadcaster, who realises now that the podcast revolution really is here to stay, and that listeners can enjoy audio programmes that are exactly relating to their own interests on demand, and don't have to wait until a broadcaster puts programmes in their schedules, and what's more there is no limit of a programme's duration, unlike on a radio station!

So I am pretty confident that I will have you all covered, and you are of course welcome to flip around the sections and get the information in a different order if you wish, please be my guest!

I'll take your hand through all the various stages of creating the content, setting out your recording area at home or in your office, getting the equipment you need, doing the recordings both with yourself presenting and you interviewing others, then I'll show you how to quickly and professionally edit your podcasts and upload them to various platforms.

I'll also show you how to optimise your content using metadata such as ID3 tags, so people can find your podcasts easier and get a bigger following. I'll also show you how to use the many new online platforms that help with podcast marketing and monitoring, and how to make an income from your podcasts. Also I'll give my advice on setting up a dedicated Podcast production company.

My name is Peter Baker, and I have been in the audio production business for more than 40 years including working at the BBC, ITV, and very many radio stations in the UK and Austria and countless podcast projects, so you can really have confidence that what I tell you will be very useful, practical, and has a stamp of authority!

You may like to check out the other training courses of ours that have thousands of students at www.VoiceoverMasterclass.com

The great thing about podcasts is that you can zone in on a single topic and get on board all sorts of fans who also love the same subject.   Podcast listening round the world has accelerated enormously over recent years, and the rise is seeing no sign of flattening off.

When you see national radio broadcasters like the BBC now putting so many resources into creating podcasts, rather than traditional radio programmes that have to go out at a certain time and day, and that have a fixed and inflexible duration, you know you're onto a winner!

Podcasts are great for hobby or lifestyle subjects but, they can also be important for an organizations and businesses that want to share regular updates with their clients or people interested in what they're doing. In fact, if you are creating a podcast for your business, it will help differentiate your brand from others enormously.

As you'll appreciate, marketing is becoming ever more competitive, and for your brand to stand out from the rest becomes harder as time goes by. So podcasts offer a fresh personal experience, and you can get ahead of your competition, who may only be sending out the odd pdf newsletter or a quarterly printed magazine that you're not quite sure is read – or if it's just left on the coffee table.

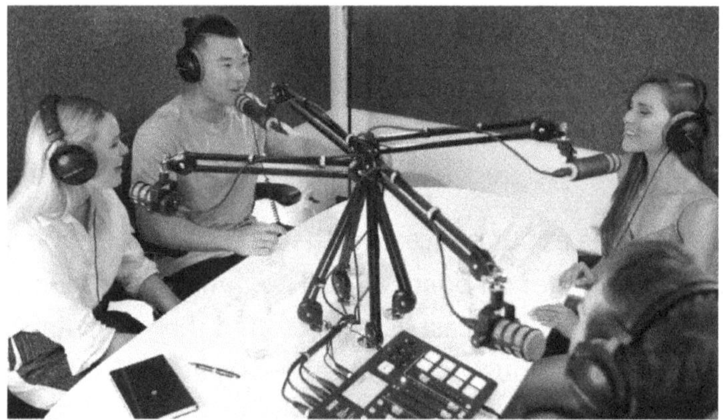

Podcasts, of course, use the internet so they reach people around the world, and there have been so many podcasters who have made a load of new contacts and friends in other countries and businesses who now have expanded their horizons.

Now, it doesn't matter what your set-up budget is or what your podcast is going to be about. I'll make sure that you'll get your equipment together; I'll teach you how to present with confidence and to record and produce a finished professional podcast.

I'll take you through the whole process and how to submit your podcast to the most popular podcast directories like Apple Podcasts, Stitcher, Google Play, Spotify, and so on, and also we'll give you essential detailed information to show you how you can rank well in the podcast directories and give advice on the all-important graphic "thumbnail" that needs to go with every podcast, so it captures people's attention when they're scrolling through the directory.

OVERVIEW OF THE PODCASTING PROCESS

Let's have a quick overview of the whole production process, before we dive into each area in great detail. I assume that you know the niche or the subject area that you want to create your podcast around, and you've got some great creative ideas when it comes to who will co-present with you, where you going to record it and also the kind of features that you go to have, and we'll discuss this in a lot more detail later on.

I assume that you want to record in your own home facility, I won't be so grand to call it a studio, but it'll feel a bit like that to you, and the great thing is that these days you can have some really good quality recording equipment that doesn't cost that much. They key to quality recording at home or in an office is to find a very quiet location that is acoustically "dead" – in other words minimal sound reflections or echo.

Every presenter should have their own microphone and you may need a mixer as well. Every microphone needs to have a holder, ideally an adjustable boom arm with a shock mount and also a pop filter to stop nasty speech plosive sounds.

Then you'll need some audio software to do the editing and to mix it all together. If you're already a voice over artist, maybe you already have Adobe Audition, but if you don't want to spend money on Adobe Audition, then Audacity or WavePad would be fine. For interviews, you may want to use Skype or Zoom, but I really recommend Riverside.fm or Cleanfeed.net which makes things easy for podcasters, and we have a whole section on that later on. I'll also show you later on various "all-in-one" podcast studios which can act as mixers and recorders and editors, so you may prefer to buy one of these.

Once your studio and recording solution is sorted out, and you have the details of your first podcast in your mind, you'll need to develop the details about it and how it'll sound to the world.

So, imagine you've got a podcast listing magazine. You need to sit down and write out a selling line about it. Think about who it's aimed at, and what they want to hear. What problems would it help solve for them? Then write a paragraph about it in your imaginary listing magazine. Actually, when you upload your finished file, you'll need to fill in a lot of information anyway, so think about it beforehand, and it will save you a lot of grief and time later.

You'll need a good intelligent snappy podcast title, that is relevant to your podcast. You also need a subtitle. This is simply a one-line description of your show , probably who it's aimed at, or what its actual aim is. Then you'll need to think of some keywords - 5 to 7 main keywords related to your podcast topic so that people can find your podcast easily when they search. Your description can also have keywords in. And don't forget the all-important podcast artwork file - a 3000 by 3000 pixel image file, which you can get designed for you or you can easily do yourself for free and I'll tell you how later.

Before you start recording your first episode, you need to at least title out a whole series. This way, you won't be a one hit wonder, and you'll have plenty to talk about on that first programme as you can highlight the things that your listeners can look forward to. So get a diary, and write down various topic ideas that still keep you within your niche.

And also think of ideas for potential guests to interview on your show. The great thing about the internet, is of course that your guests can be anywhere in the world. This is not like "Wayne's World", where your guests have to physically come down to your basement! They can be anywhere, and I'll tell you how to get guests to come on your programme easily, and the best way to interview them. For the actual recording itself, you need to do some practise recordings first, to make sure that you and your fellow presenters if there are any, know what they are doing, and that technically everything works OK.

EDITING:
- A creative process
- Put things in a different order
- Cut out mistakes
- Improve audio quality
- Add in music and SFX if relevant

Then after the main recording, you then do your editing. Probably, you would have recorded any interviews on different days, so this needs to be edited into the main studio recording. This is a fun thing to do, and it is quite easy to get to learn how to edit things together. You can be creative, with different jingles or music or sound effects if it's relevant, but the great thing is when it comes to duration of your programmes, the world of the podcast is as long as it is long. Unlike radio programmes which have to be stuffed into a fixed time, it's up to you to decide when it gets boring, or when a discussion or an interview can go on a bit more. In editing as well as taking out mistakes, repetition, and things that aren't that relevant, you can put things in different orders, and also insert features and other materials until you are fully happy with it.

last

thing you do, is to check the audio levels. You don't want your listeners to continually turn up and down their volume do you? So you can either do this yourself manually, altering levels and adding compression, or use one of the online services, like **Auphonic.com**. this is where you upload your finished file, and it evens out the levels, and also can clean up any light background noise if you wish. After the editing, you then prepare the file and export the podcast as an MP3 file. This is quite a small file, but the quality will be fine for a podcast export. Then you would upload your episodes, but it's not to the places that you think! You need a media host, and that isn't Apple podcasts and so on.

There are many media hosts you can select, for example BuzzSprout is a very popular one. You would be registered there, and you would log in, and enter the information into the podcast show settings.

You would add your podcast artwork, and you would set up your feed with your podcast details. Then you upload the actual MP3 audio file and you get sent an RSS code. With this, you can either publish it immediately to directories, or you can schedule your episode to publish at a later date.

You would go to Apple podcasts, and submit the podcast feed , in other words the magic link, that your host has given you. You can also submit your podcast to other podcast directory's, such as Stitcher, Spotify, Pandora, Deezer and iHeartRadio. Don't forget Google Podcasts, although it should happen automatically through your website after Google finds it has been published on your site, with that link from your podcast host.

At the same time, you really ought to have a website as well to support your show, to actually display more details about your team, and to have comprehensive "show notes" about each of your episodes. Here you would capture search engine traffic and build your email list from your podcast and provide additional supplemental information that supports your podcast, with links to various suppliers that you may have mentioned on your podcast.

PODCAST WEBSITE
Podcast details
Team biogs
Episode show notes
SEO Capture
Build your email list
Links to info and sites mentioned in episodes
A place for newbies to podcasts to listen

You would also have a facility for listening to every podcast episode on your website, because there are still an awful lot of people who don't understand how you pick up podcasts, thinking it's kind of a radio station thing.

Now, don't laugh, we were all ignorant at one point weren't we! So, the website is extremely important, and you can embed a "media play" link from your podcast host so people can play the episode directly from your website, or download the MP3 themselves if you want. There are still some people, who like to have the actual MP3 file, to put on a USB memory stick, which they put in a car for long journeys. Yes, people still do that! And unless you address the needs of all possible types of listeners generally, you will miss out on a lot of listeners.

So once your programme is on air, so to speak, how are you going to get people to listen to it? Well, we have this covered in a huge way later on, when we come to the many ways to promote your podcasts.

CHOOSING A NICHE

The following is reproduced from a Buzzsprout help screen:

Note: Is your podcast already listed in Apple Podcasts?

If you just moved to Buzzsprout and already have an Apple Podcasts listing, you do not need to resubmit. You should check out this help article instead.

Step 1: Review your podcast info for the Apple Podcasts required fields

The following fields are required to submit your podcast to Apple Podcasts:

- Title
- Description
- Artwork
- Category (at least 1)
- Language
- Explicit or not

Step 2: Submit your RSS feed to Apple Podcasts

Click the button below to submit your RSS feed to Apple Podcasts.

This section is called "choosing a niche", and I'll go through the main categories and subcategories of podcasts as determined by the all-important directory of Apple Podcasts.

You may not feel this section relevant to you if you know exactly what you want to cover, for example you are totally passionate at one particular area in your life and you want to tell the world about it and discuss it with your colleagues on the podcast who are just as crazy about it!

Or maybe you are creating a podcast for your own company or organisation, so you're not actually looking for a type of niche to promote. However, you could be a radio producer with a wide range of interests and like to know what the possibilities are for focusing on a certain subject that would be successful as a podcast.

Most podcasts that are successful are hosted and produced by people who are very experienced about the subject matter, and have got many relevant contacts as well, so it's easy for them to find interviewees, and also means that if you are in that particular niche with your work or your interests or your experience in life, it's much easier to think of various topics for each week's subject. And that's what you're aiming towards really.

PODCAST DIRECTORIES
Apple podcasts
Spotify
Google podcasts
TuneIn Radio (Amazon)
Stitcher
Pandora
iHeart Radio
Podchaser
Radio Public
Castbox
iPodder
Deezer
Player FM

General subject podcasts that are basically hosted by someone who talks about general lifestyle issues really aren't that successful unless you're a celebrity already, or you get a break where your personality shines through and people latch on to what you are saying, you become an influencer and your podcast gains traction.

Essentially, if you produce a podcast, you really need to be continually in the zone of the subject matter, and as an example I'd mention not one of my productions, but a couple who produce a podcast that I personally subscribe to.   Nic Redman and Leah Marks are professional voice talents, and that's a hat I wear as well, and I'm in their social club and their podcast called THE VO SOCIAL has been going for some years now, and every month there's a completely different subject that they cover.

Now if you're not a voice over, you may think what an earth could they be talking about? Just whining about not getting enough work or rates of pay, probably? Well actually, thinking about all the subjects that have been covered, that hasn't even been mentioned at all yet! If you think a voice over sits at home read scripts and gets paid for them and that's the end of the matter, well no, it's a big industry, with an awful lot to talk about, and so when you dig deep, and think about all the aspects that are related to the industry, it's amazing what you come up with, that are actually riveting subjects to people who live and breathe for that niche.

Topics have included, how to cope if you're asked to scream a script for a voiceover; the concerns that AI computer voices will take over the work of human voiceovers; what voice coaches actually do, how to get more work in gaming, what the "Mid-Atlantic" accent really is, the work of a studio engineer, awards ceremony Voice Of God techniques and so on. If you think you're ever going to be stuck for a subject for a niche, and that's after Googling subjects and looking at what's in the niche's trade and consumer press, well, it's not a good niche, or you haven't looked hard enough!

So I hope that has given you an idea of how you can get a basic niche and drill down to get even more detailed, and if you feel there is a market for it, that's where your podcast journey can begin.

I think it's useful to go through the list of categories that Apple Podcasts ask you to put your own productions into. At the time of recording, there are 19 overall categories, and most of these are broken into subcategories. When you've finished with the editing of each episode of your podcast and send it up for submission to Apple, via your host service, you need to choose an overall category as your own primary category, and you can't just leave that section of the form blank, even if you have thought of a very bizarre subject, that you think cannot be categorised! So just have a think about where your ideas and hopes and dreams for a successful podcast fit in this list.

First of all there's arts, and this section contains subsections on books, design, fashion and beauty, food, performing arts, and visual arts.

The second category is business. This category also has subcategories of careers, entrepreneurship, investing, management, marketing, and also non-profit businesses.

The third category is comedy, you realise these are now in alphabetical order don't you! The comedy section has subsections on comedy interviews, improvisation, and stand-up podcasts.

The 4th category in Apple podcasts is education. This contains courses , how to type podcasts, language learning, and self-improvement.

The 5th category is fiction, and this contains comedy fiction, drama and science fiction.

The sixth category is government, and there are no subcategories on this particular one, I'm not sure whether that's a good or a bad thing! Would your podcast niche be somewhere in Government?

Let's move onto category #7, which is health and fitness. This category contains subcategories of alternative health, fitness, medicine, mental health, nutrition and sexuality.

Category #8 in Apple podcast is history, and there are no subcategories there.

Category 9 is called kids and family. Here you can choose a subcategory of education for kids, parenting, pets and animals, and also storeys for kids.

 The 10th category has the title of leisure. This contains animation and manga, automotive, aviation, crafts, games , hobbies, home and garden , video games. Now just off the top of my head I can think of other categories that would go under leisure, but as I say you have to select the closest possible to your own niche, as you cannot leave the section blank when you upload your podcast and try and get it in the Apple directory.

The 11th category is music. With subcategories music commentary music history and music interviews.

The 12th category is news coma and maybe your podcast would be a general news theme, or you could choose a subcategory of business news, Daily News, entertainment news, news commentary, politics , Sports News, or tech news.

The 13th category is religion and spirituality, which contains Buddhism, Christianity, Hinduism, Islam, Judaism, religion, and spirituality.

The 14th category is science, that contains astronomy, chemistry, earth Sciences, life Sciences, mathematics, natural Sciences, nature, physics, and social Sciences. Category 15 is called society and culture. This has subcategories of documentary, personal journals, philosophy, places and travel, and relationships.

Category 16 is sports, and even though there are many more sports than there are subcategories, you either have to choose the sports main category or choose one of the following sub categories, which are baseball, basketball, cricket, fantasy sports, football, golf, hockey, rugby, running, soccer, swimming, tennis , volleyball, wilderness , and wrestling.

Category 17 is simply called technology with no subcategories.

Category 18 is called true crime, as against fiction crime, that would go under category 5, and finally category 19 is called TV and film. This has subcategories of after shows, film history, film interviews, film reviews, and TV reviews.

At the time of putting this together, Statista USA has listed the most popular category with 22% of the pie to comedy, this is followed by various news podcasts, then true crime, sport, health and fitness, religion and faith, politics, self-help, investigative journalism, fitness, then scripted drama at the end with 8%. But stats change all the time, countries listening habits change as well, so there's no point giving you exact figures here, but there's one thing for sure, and that the podcast phenomenon is here to stay, and listeners are going up all the time. And they're going up a lot. If I was asked to invest in a new talk radio station or put an investment into podcasts, podcasts would definitely win;

the world has really changed.   As I have mentioned
before, when national radio broadcasters around the
world are now putting so many resources into creating
podcasts, rather than traditional programmes that go out
at a certain time and day, and that have a fixed and
inflexible duration, you know you're onto a winner!

Now, there's no point in finding a really empty category
and putting your podcast in there if it's actually about a
completely different subject. It will get rejected anyway.
But your podcast primary category really matters it
determines the company you keep within the podcast
ecosystem. Ideally you should choose a specific
subcategory if one exists as that will help gain traction
with listeners.

So, if you're an all-rounder, interested in producing
podcasts on anything that you could create an interest for,
and then you'd go and find the experts, what niche would
you select? You could either go for the categories that are
extremely popular, and fight the competition there, or go
for a category that isn't popular, and build it into a big
hitter with less competition! I think the old adage saying
"if you want to stand out from the crowd, **understand** the
crowd".

Once you're happy with the general niche that you want to go down with for your proposed podcast episodes, now it's time to do a little bit more thinking.

First of all, you need to look at the competition for that particular niche, and see what past episodes they have covered, and you just need to listen to them. Some of them will be very good and you can hope to join them on the upper rungs of quality and content soon, and some of them will be pretty poor, both in terms of content and technical quality.

For the good ones you find, don't be put off completely by thinking that you could never compete with a show like this, because they had to start somewhere, didn't they? But what about the bad podcasts you discover? Maybe the actual editorial would be fine, if some of the annoying aspects could be taken out of the way, so try and work out why people are listening to the bad ones; is it something they are putting up with, in order to enjoy the material that they want?

In other words, if you could offer people the same material, but without some of the annoying aspects, like without very poor technical quality and audio distortion or echo, or simply the presenters chatting amongst themselves and messing around, that's where you can go in there and create a more professional version of what they're offering.

Once you've listened to the competition, you need to develop your angle on the podcast niche. And it could be a subcategory of a subcategory, that could sustain for a whole series or even a continuous podcast series.

I think it's important for you to set goals for your podcast. What do you want it to achieve? Is it an organisational or corporate push, is it something to keep staff involved and informed about what's going on at the organisation, or is it a simple hobby podcast, where it doesn't really matter if not that many people are listening, and you are quite happy with a small audience but one that is appreciative?

It could be that you want it to be a money spinner, and you want it to grow, and win awards, and generate a full-time income for you, and that is fine as well, but unless you have got goals to begin with, it's very difficult to put things in place to achieve those goals.

Next you need to look at your audience, try and understand their own interests and needs, by searching the Internet. Look at Facebook groups, and see questions people are asking about your subject in Quora or Redditt. If it's a company podcast you're going to do, talk to your colleagues, and see what they want from a potential podcast that you are thinking of putting together. Again if they don't understand what a podcast is, just say it's like a radio show, that's just aimed at them. Listen to people, and then at the end make decisions based on three things:

> a) **the input from people you are spoken to,**
> b) **from data that you can find easily and openly on the Internet and**
> c) **your gut feeling!**

Next the name of your podcast name is really important; it needs to be a catchy and memorable name, and obviously not one that you've just stolen from an already successful podcast. Note what you would put down as the main title, a subtitle, the author, and the description tags. It might be that one of the description tags could actually be a better name than what you thought of already.

The title must be specific to boost appearance in relevant searches. Try and avoid a long title or main name for your podcast. Don't just try to stuff keywords into a long title just because you can, as it will work against you in the main scheme of things.

You need to create a premise for your show; in other words, are you going to be relating news, are you going to be reviewing things, is it homage to something, or are you there to complain and try and right wrongs with something, is it a campaign of some sort? Whatever premise you select, it needs to be consistent throughout the series, you can't just change premise mid-stream!

You need a name that reflects the tone and mood of the podcast, and don't call it something really obscure and hope it will take off, because it probably won't, and it may well get rejected by platforms if you have a surreal title. Also don't use any abusive terms or words, as this will get rejected. Once you have decided on a name, then determine the keywords that can be generated from that name.

In other words, you would find a keyword generator, such as the one that Google gives you free for Google Ads, and write down as many keywords as you can so that when people are searching for those words, they may find you, and your podcast. These will be useful not just for the description that you need to write when you submit a podcast, but for all the text that you have on your website, in various sections, and also keywords are so important to keep a podcast editorially on course, in the right direction.

After the title, you need to create a compelling description of your podcast, and that will also optimise your title in the search engines, you are only usually allowed 4000 characters, so you can't write an essay, but try and get some of the main keywords in there, that will help people to find you.

Next you need to do a little thinking about who's going to host the podcast. Is it going to be just yourself? Are you going to have a co-host, or even a zoo type format, where it's all buzzing and people are talking over each other? Or will that just annoy? It all depends on your proposed target audience!

If you are thinking of having a co-host, be aware that this only works, if there's a good chemistry between the two presenters. The best duo presenter teams seem to have a sixth sense as to what the other is thinking and know when they're about to start talking and end talking.

If you're not sure who is going to present, or how many presenters you are going to have, then just record some demos, and be honest with each other as to whether you think it works better with two, three or simply a single presenter.   It can get annoying to listeners sometimes, when there's just a cacophony of voices, and people are just messing about, and talking about things in the studio or the colour of the curtains, the taste of the coffee or anything not relevant when you just want to hear some solid content. If you do have three or four people who want to be involved, then have a main presenter, and give the other people specific jobs where they're just talking on their own.

They could present a feature like "Review of the week", or "feedback from listeners" from last week, or "here's our gadget of the week", or "idea of the week". Having specific features with different voices, often helps the flow of a podcast, so experiment until you get the balance just right. Record, playback, analyse. That's so important before you launch a podcast. Be honest with each other and it won't all end in tears , and you'll know you'll have the most talented presenters in the right positions.

So what else do you need to think about? Well, you need to select a podcast host. No, this isn't the presenter of the show, we're not talking about that kind of host, it's a provider you subscribe to where you actually upload your finished files to, and then you get an RSS feed to get yourself placed on the various directories.

You also need work out the directories you wish to be featured on, and much more on this later.   But what you will also need to do is to create a website dedicated to your podcast. If the title of your podcast can be incorporated into the URL, or the web address, all the better.

 It's not the end of the world though if you can't get the exact name to match your podcast title. Your listeners will be the ones who will be directed to that website, and you won't find many people just discovering your website randomly unless you're very lucky.

On this website, which you can create yourself easily, via WIX.com or many other website creation platforms out there, you can easily insert not just a straight audio listen

29

feature for all your past podcasts, but you can install podcast plugins so that when people click on that they can find the directory straight away.

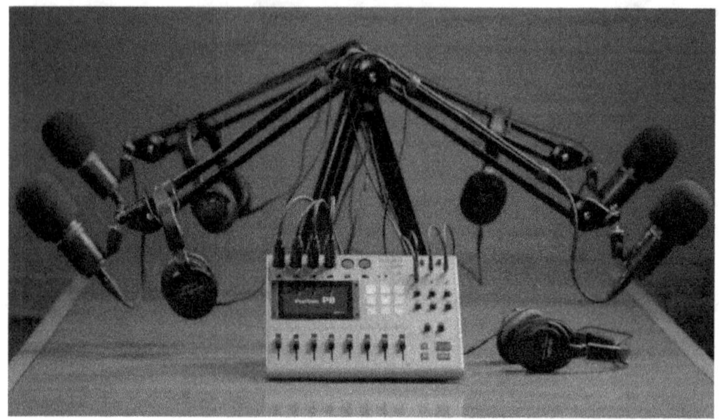

If you don't fancy the hassle of doing this, you could use a service like **radiopublic.com** who offer custom so-called "**podsites**" specially designed for podcasters like us. More on this service later.

I cannot overemphasise that even though podcasts are big in OUR heads and we're talking about them all the time, there is a huge untapped potential of audience out there, even computer literate and tech savvy people, who don't really understand what a podcast is and where to find them.

So you can certainly direct people first of all from existing social media or other ways to contact people to your dedicated website, and they can listen on the website in the traditional way.

But the podcast plugin will give them a link to where your podcast is found on directories, and they can subscribe to you on that, and knew podcast fans can be generated, with yours as their very first subscription. It's very exciting to be able to introduce someone to a new podcast and they like you enough to subscribe, and then from there it's onwards and upwards!

PODCAST STRUCTURE

As we have mentioned before, it is important for each podcast to have a specific theme, a focus, some topic that runs throughout the podcast. But – assume you are planning to have a weekly podcast - that's not to say that there can't be some regular features that aren't to do with that week's subject. For example, probably you might want to consider having a roundup of feedback from last week's topic.

You would find some comments from your listeners who agree or disagree with what was said on the last podcast, and you would gauge reaction to see if it's worth visiting that topic again.

You may wish to have a competition, an interesting fact of the week, a gadget of the week or something like that which is not to do with the main theme, and that is fine. It's really important to try and keep the same **structure** every week though, and you can create a template, either as a Word document or a printed piece of paper, where you have a box for each section that needs to be completed.

You could start with the introduction Jingle, the welcome and menu, then the main topic Part 1, and then some industry news, then Part 2 of the subject, the main interview, last week's feedback and so on. The structure will of course be determined by the niche and your own research for the target audience. But try and keep the same every episode to create a feeling of familiarity.

One thing you won't have to worry about, unlike a broadcast radio programme, is the duration. It lasts as long as it lasts on a podcast. If you feel the subject has run its course get together, finish it there. If you feel something is running over and things are being repeated in the conversation, or in the interview, well you know what to do don't you? Interestingly in various surveys of podcast fans, it seems that people "lose themselves" in them so much when they're listening that they don't realise that time is going by. They are so engrossed in the material and in the conversation, that an hour or so has gone by... but if you asked them how long they've been listening they might say 20 or 30 minutes! That's the power of the podcast for you!

If you are running out of ideas for topics, and you find that the feedback from the listeners doesn't exactly help, then spend some time researching websites and social media on your particular topic, and you might want to subscribe to various YouTube channels and follow people on Twitter who may have something interesting to say that could be topical and valid for that week's main theme. You're not exactly stealing things from them, in fact if you find a fascinating guest that is suitable for your podcast niche, contact them and get them on.

You may drive yourself crazy trying to find a topical theme for each episode. But there is absolutely nothing wrong, however, with creating a theme that is not topical at all. In fact, I would recommend that you create a standby programme, that is timeless. You would keep this "on the shelf", in case you became ill, or wanted to go on a vacation, or you had a family emergency, or anything else that meant you needed a podcast episode that was already created fast!

If you have got listeners tuned into you, and are salivating like Pavlov's dog waiting for the day of the email to arrive to say that your new podcast was available, then you don't want to disappoint them. So always keep an emergency episode that has no topical material in it at all, for that special occasion.

WEEKLY PRODUCTION SCHEDULE

Day 1 - research

Day 2 - writing / recording insert items

Day 3 - script writing for intro / outro & details

Day 4 - Rehearsal and recording

Day 5 - Editing & mastering

Day 6 - Checking and uploading to podcast host

Once you get into your stride of podcast production, you'll find it so useful to have a day dedicated mostly to one thing. If you have a weekly podcast, then you could have the first day to determine the theme for next week, the 2nd day to sort out the items that are regular, the 3rd day putting any script together, although I'm sure much of it will be ad-libbed and conversation, the 4th day could be recording, the 5th they would be editing and listening back, and then you would release your podcast on the 6th day. Giving you a day of rest before it all starts again. Of course, everyone will be different, and you will find that things change, but if you have some sort of structure in your diary, it helps things to get done!

No matter how good you are as a presenter and a fount of all knowledge, a podcast is much more interesting when you are having a discussion with somebody else. You will often find that a conversation between people can be listened to for longer, it makes it more enjoyable. No matter how much you think you are an expert on a subject, there is always someone who knows more and a guest to be interviewed on your podcast each episode would normally be a great boost to the sound of it and to the enjoyment and appreciation by your listeners. You may be able to get the expert to come to your studio, but it's much more likely that it'd be a remote interview, so that's what's considered here and in the next section about the technical considerations.

Experts who are approached by journalists, often say "no" to an interview, because of the hassle factor. A journalist from a newspaper or a magazine may take half an hour or so on the phone just to get a few quotes for their article, and the expert may also be worried about whether the quote will be accurate or taken out of context. When you are interviewing them via Zoom or Skype or any other system, it only takes the time you want them on microphone, although you could always edit them down afterwards.

And also they know that their voice will be the only thing you take so they won't usually sound like they are speaking out of context, unless you're really nasty to them in the edit suite! So normally, experts like to be on podcasts, and if they especially like to be on podcasts if they are promoting something of their own, whether it's a service, their new book, some research they have done or anything else they are involved in. Usually, you will find experts very willing to take part in your podcast. So, what is the best way to go about it?

If the expert you want to interview is working for an organization, whether it's a big business or a university or the government, you need to go through the press department. Explain what your podcast is about, and the angle you are taking on that particular episode of your podcast and why you want to speak to your expert. It's always best to go through a press department at an organization, rather than just ring up reception and insist on talking to the expert direct. You will get much more cooperation and your interviewee will be much more likely to take part, if it's all agreed by the organisation's press department, and they may even offer some extra help or offer other interviewees who might assist you for future episodes.

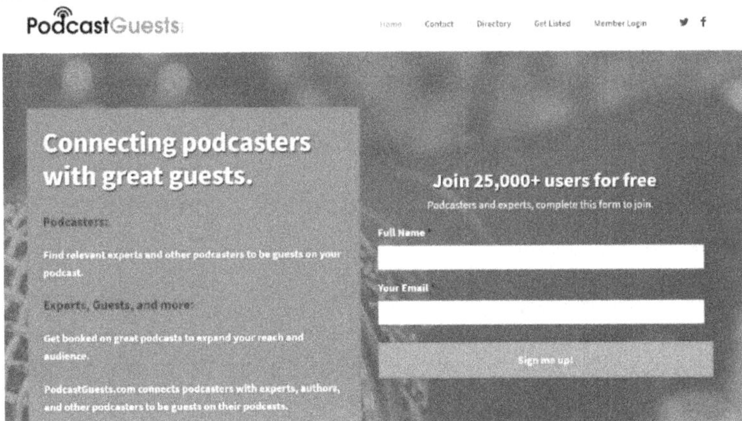

So what if you can't find relevant guests for your podcasts? Why not check out **PodcastGuests.com**? This site connects podcasters with experts, authors, and other podcasters to be guests on their podcasts.

If you're a podcaster, the site will find relevant experts and other podcasters to be guests on your podcast, you just explain what type of guest you're seeking. Other podcasters and experts apply to be on your show. **PodcastGuests.com** shares the list of interested guests with you.

For the experts, they fill out a simple form to apply to relevant podcasts.

So check out **podcastguests.com**, it could be very handy for you when you're starting out, before you get a regular group of experts and guests you'll work with!

Here's a quick check list of what you need to sort out with any expert or guest before recording:

The correct spelling of their name and their title.

How to pronounce the guest's name if you're not sure

Their email address

Their phone number (in case something comes up last minute)

Their web site URL

A photo to be placed on the promo page of your podcast website

A brief biography about their background

The name & URL to any products or services they plan to discuss.

The URL to their affiliate program so you can promote their products/services.

When you make contact with your expert, make sure that they are going to do the interview for free. Most people will be perfectly happy to do this, but sometimes there are charges, or you may be obliged to give a donation to a charity. But once this has been sorted and also a time agreed which should be really at their convenience and not yours, then an email confirmation should be sent explaining more about what you want them to do, maybe a list of questions, but certainly the line of enquiry you wish to take, and also the connection link or any other technical connection information by email.

More about this in the next section.

Without being too prescriptive, and doing it in a friendly manner, request that they do the interview with you in a quiet room with soft furnishings around, so there is minimal echo, and ask if they have a "clip on" lapel microphone, or a headphone microphone, that will give better quality then using the one that's built into their laptop or webcam which could be a few feet away from their mouth on a shiny reflective desk!

You hope to get a reply back that will put your mind at rest, knowing the recording is all sorted to be recorded. Even though the podcast is audio, we do suggest that you use a video medium like Zoom or Skype for the initial contact chat as it is much more personable, and friendly, when you see the other person's face. Then sort out the actual interview details which could be done audio only to optimise the audio quality on any slow internet connections in the chain. Of course if you are using riverside.fm (explained later, you can have great audio quality and still have video, no matter if the internet speed is terrible!)

A friendly reminder email a few hours before the actual main recording can be useful. When you first make connection with your expert for your interview, make sure you do some small talk at the beginning and explain that you aren't recording yet, in case there are some new things that the expert wants to say that they don't want to come across on your podcast. And then when you're ready, explain clearly that you are recording now – things will go "on the record" - and off you go. If you happen to speak over each other or if you want the expert to repeat something, maybe because something has cut out technically or you genuinely didn't understand their reply, then you are the host and you need to ask them to repeat what they have just said or just ask the question again; you're not live on air, so don't worry. It can be sorted in edit later!

Remember, it's your podcast and you just have to act like a professional radio presenter in being genuinely interested in what your guest is saying and ask questions related to what they have said. This is very important. If you've ever listened to a radio program with an inexperienced presenter, it can be very frustrating when the guest is obviously just being asked a list of questions that have been typed out on the presenter's screen or piece of paper, and it's obvious they haven't been listening to the answers.

So, yes, of course, have a list of questions, but use them as a guide - but simply LISTEN! You may find the flow of conversation takes a completely different course to what you had in mind when you wrote your initial list of questions. Bear in mind that you will edit everything afterwards, so don't worry if there's a long gap after an answer before you think of the next appropriate question as this can easily be cut out in edit afterwards.

 It's better to leave a gap than to talk over your guest, which will sound horrible if it can't be edited out.

If it's an extended interview and the guest knows this, there's no problem stopping the recording and having a break for a drink and a chat, but just make it clear when you ARE recording for the formal interview and when you are just chatting.

This is an old trick played by political journalists, by the way. The journalist implies they have stopped recording, but really are still recording and hoping to get a juicy quote from a politician when their guard is down at the break, but I don't suggest you go down this route or even need to think about this!

After your interview has finished recording, send a thank you email to your guest speaker.

When it's been edited, email again and include the link to the recording and transcripts and ask them to share it with their followers.

To finish this section, with interviews, there are three basic points you can take away:

1. Do Your Research
Knowing as much as possible about the expert you're going to interview is vital to producing engaging, unique interviews.
Remember, if your interviewee is well-known, they've probably been asked the same questions many times. This means that fans will have no reason to listen to yet another version of the standard interview.

However, if you research your subject's background, study their previous interviews, and take a genuine interest in their business, you'll be able to produce unique questions that serve as an excellent attraction for your customers, and other interviewees.

2. Write questions, but don't forget to LISTEN!
Great interviewers ask great questions. Come up with a standard list questions, and then cross off the obvious ones. Replace the overly generic ones with unusual and interviewee specific queries. Keep in mind that, as the interview progresses, you'll need to develop follow-up questions because you'll be LISTENING! If you've done your research, this will be easy, especially as you gain podcasting experience.

3. Have a Conversation
Want to get your guest to open up? Treat your podcast as a conversation, this is not the Spanish Inquisition and you're not a detective trying to get a confession! Listen to the best talk radio hosts, and see how they interview

people. You'll find they do this in a nice relaxed manner, listening to everything they say, it shouldn't sound like there's an obvious list of questions either written down, or in the head of the presenter. It takes a while to learn to get this right, but it's important to try and strive for a nice relaxed conversation with your guest. This is the way to get the best from them, and they'll appreciate it very much. So will your listeners!   So what are the technical considerations for recording interviews remotely? That's what we'll be covering next.

RECORDING PODCAST GUESTS - SOFTWARE AND CLOUD SOLUTIONS

So how are you going to record your podcast? There are various ways, and you can split them up into two categories. First of all, you can use software on a computer, or you can also record them on various cloud solutions, in other words things are recorded via the internet. We'll cover that in this section, and then secondly in the next section we'll look at some hardware solutions including some nifty all-in-one devices designed especially for the podcast market.

If you're a bit technophobic and worried about the recording and editing side, I have to say that, honestly, to record and edit a basic podcast isn't really that complicated at all. If it's just yourself and a colleague or two recording in one place, it is straightforward. You just need to select software that can record and edit, such as Adobe Audition which you pay for, and Audacity which is free and asks for donations or NCH Wavepad that is free for personal use.

RECORDING AND EDITING

1) Record everything (in a rough order if it needs to be)

2) Edit - put things in the right order

3) Cut out mistakes

4) Get levels and audio quality right

5) Export audio as an mp3 podcast!

You can if you want to, record everything on a basic audio recorder, and there are many really inexpensive but good quality solid state recorders around. You can record all you like on one of these devices, then transfer the files to a computer to edit.

But to be honest, why not save time and record everything on the computer that you are going to edit on anyway? You can still use your solid-state recorder as a backup device if you like, just in case the recording on the computer doesn't come out the way you had hoped.

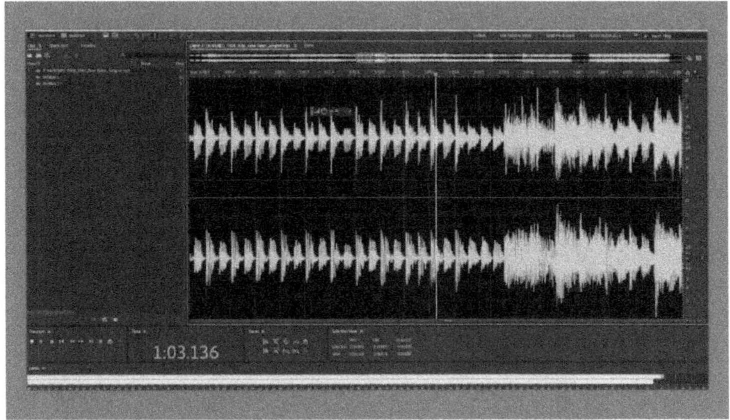

Most software programs that can record and edit audio are pretty similar. You connect your microphones to the computer either directly if they are USB microphones, or via an interface box if they are analogue microphones, and the software is made to select these microphones to record. I'll go through the technical connections and the selection of hardware in great detail later on.

Then once the software senses the microphones, you simply click the record button and off you go. You see the waveform in the middle window here. You get one waveform for a mono recording, or two waveforms above each other if it's a stereo recording - one for the left and one for the right channel. Once you've finished recording, you push stop, usually the space bar and save the file.

Then in the same software you can highlight features you don't want on the waveforms by clicking and dragging and releasing the mouse and click the delete button, you can cut and paste from other files just like you can do with a Word document and move audio around in any order you like. You can also boost levels, remove background hiss if it's there, add special effects or do all sorts of clever things.

You can use the multitrack section of your software, to layer multiple tracks to play together, for example you can mix in a music bed underneath you if you wanted it, or you can add sound effects and things like this. You can adjust the sound levels and then export a final mix with everything at the right levels for your listeners to enjoy.

So that's fine, if everything is going to take place in one location. But doing that for every episode is going to limit the kinds of things you are going to cover. You'll really need to have a good system to record guests, who are usually in different places around the planet.

Because the people you interview are going to be an important part of your programme, the technical quality needs to be good. You can't just hold up a phone to the microphone for example! So, let's take a look at how you are going to record interviews when people are in various places around the world.

If you are recording individuals or maybe a group of people in different places as podcast guests, a system like Zoom, Whereby or Skype isn't that satisfactory, as not only is a lot of the internet bandwidth wasted on the video side of your conversation, which you are not going to use anyway for your podcast, so you get poor audio quality, they have automatic microphone cut out systems.

If the system senses somebody is saying something louder than the person currently speaking, it will cut out the first person and you'll only hear the louder person; I'm sure you have found this yourself, and then there is the terrible delay on some connections for Zoom-type calls as well.

But okay, you're saying, I've thought of a clever way of sorting this out! What about if we have the conversation via Zoom, Whereby or Skype, and I ask them to record at their own end in decent quality and send their quality recording to me afterwards? Well, this is what radio broadcasters have been doing for many years, even back before the days of digital.

When I worked for the BBC in the 80's, we would sometimes send a portable tape recorder round to the interviewee's house the day before, with some instructions as to how to use it. And then on the interview day, I would interview them by phone, and I would record my bits in the studio in great quality and they would also record their own contributions at decent quality at their end! Then, they would, can you believe it, post the tape back to us, or have someone from the BBC pick up the whole package! At my end, as the interviewer or the reporter, I would edit the whole lot together in good quality sound!

The modern equivalent is of course to record at their end on their phone or on a digital recorder and ask them after the interview to strip the file from their drive and sent it to you via WeTransfer.com or something to you. But you're putting the interviewee under an awful lot of stress if they're not that technical, this stress may well affect the quality of the interview, and it's a lot of hassle all round.

You may also find if you get separate recordings from people who record at their end and the recording by you at your end, that they don't match up exactly over a long interview. This is known as "audio drift", and it's due to everyone's computers having slightly different clock speeds.

So, wouldn't it be great to have a digital tool where you get good quality at the interviewer's end and also at the contributor's end where you can record quality audio without drift and without hassle?

Well, if you are an existing voice artist with your own studio, you may already have a subscription to an internet-based audio recording system, such as ipDTL, Source Connect or SessionLink Pro, where you can record good quality audio interviews over the Internet. You're welcome to try these out. Basically, you subscribe to the service and you get a link to send to the guest who usually has to have the Chrome browser installed. They enter their name once they click the link and then you get a high-quality connection for you to record the whole interview at your end.

These systems give wonderful quality; but here are three sites I'll give you that has cracked how to offer excellent quality in an experience just for us podcasters! After you've tried out any of the these following recommendations, you'll never ever do Podcast interviews again via Zoom's user-unfriendly clunky interface and usually awful audio quality even with a good internet connection!

RIVERSIDE

Let me introduce to you to Riverside.fm !

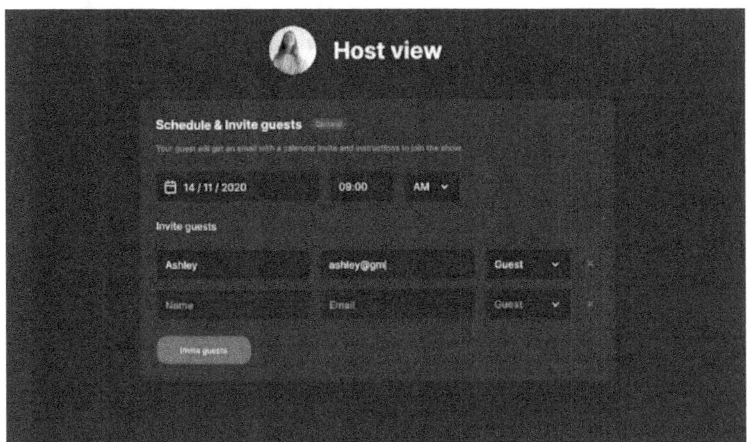

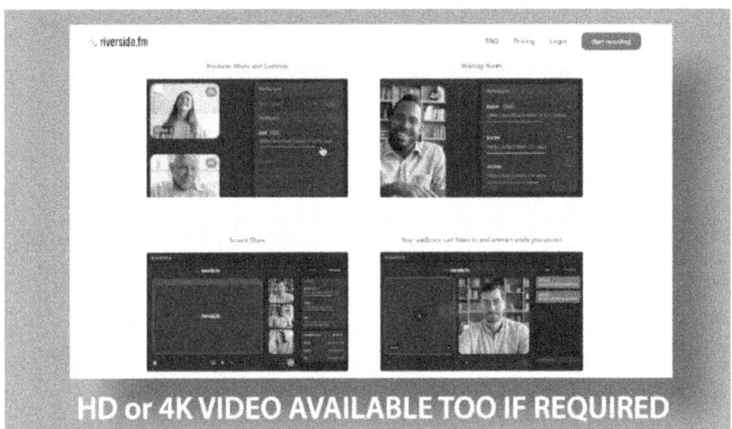

Riverside cleverly does a similar job to you asking your guests, wherever they are in the world to record at their end locally, and then they send that recording to you...but it's all done automatically. So, the recording takes place on their computer instead of over the internet. The advantage of this is that the recordings are in really high quality and after downloading the recording, you won't hear the disruptions caused by bad internet connections.

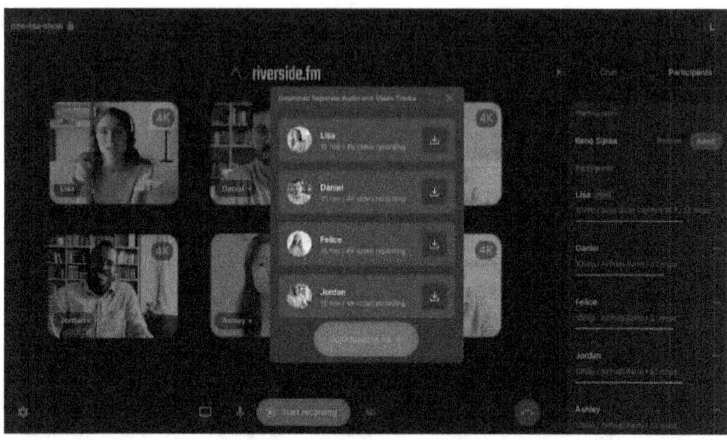

For each guest you get a separate audio track, recorded locally in pristine uncompressed wav format.

You can get 4K video as well if you want it!

Of course, the actual quality you get when you download it from your guest's end is still determined by the quality of their recording environment, the quietness of their room, and the quality of their microphone, and where that microphone is and so on, and so on! But it's absolutely makes it easy for your guest, to simply accept the recording being done on their computer at their end, via the Chrome browser that they need to have installed, and it works easily! Your guests don't need to have a Riverside account. You just send them a link and they just accept and click.

Riverside automatically uploads the local recordings from your guests during the recording so that you can download all local high-quality recordings from the participants after the podcast in minutes. You can even stop recording and continue later or another day with the same guest and it works it all out. What's more, the guest link of each podcast session is reusable, so if you wanted to record again with the same people, they could easily join the session using the same link. This is quite convenient because you can simply create a session and invite all future guests by sharing the same link every time. All the recordings you create will be saved on your Riverside dashboard. You schedule and invite your guests with **one click**. Guests and producers join with **one click.** All from your Chrome browser on laptop or desktop.

 It's really clever and it's not just audio, by the way, if you wanted to see your guests while recording, just keep the video cameras on, as even though this would normally degrade the audio signal with the reduction of the bandwidth, this only affects the audio you hear when recording. Select 4K video if you wish as long as the cameras can support or justify this resolution! After recording, you'll get the full quality files, locally recorded at the guest's end. You can even livestream your interview to Facebook, Twitter, YouTube and Twitch simultaneously, and if you wish to do this, this is included in your Riverside subscription. Riverside offers an hour free to try it out, so click away HERE and astonished!

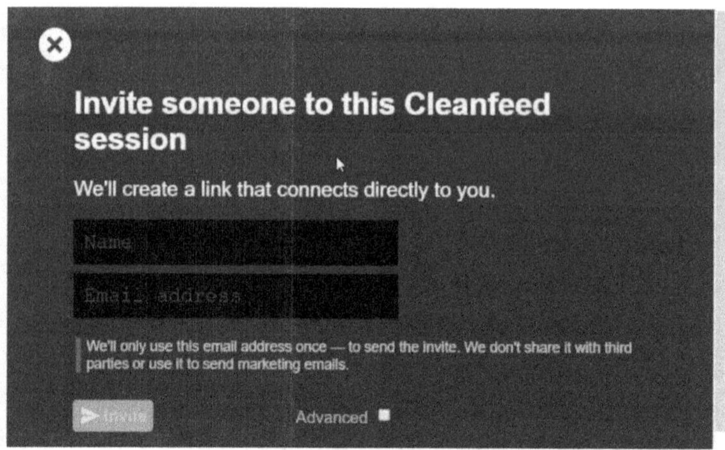

CLEANFEED

This is an audio system called <u>Cleanfeed</u>, and is free to use for a basic account. Cleanfeed was invented in the UK by Mark Hills and Marc Bakos and offers some excellent features for podcast production, especially as it records in the cloud so that side is all taken care of. The system means you don't need a mixer in the studio or have to record guests and edit in with other contributors or your own presentation later, you can do it all live if you want to.

It also runs in the Chrome browser, and you can set up guests around the world, who can talk to each other or talk to you, just like you can in a normal Zoom or Skype conversation, but the audio quality is really excellent, as long as of course, each party has a decent microphone and audio environment at their own ends. I'll go into detail about this later on.

Everybody also needs to wear headphones so there are no echo or feedback problems with loudspeakers blaring out for any contributor. Cleanfeed works by simply asking everyone to connect a decent quality microphone into their computers, either direct via USB, or via an audio interface, if the microphones are analogue.

You'd log into **Cleenfeed.net** using your username, not your email address, and give permission for Cleenfeed to use your microphone or audio device. You should see the meter move as you speak. Any issues, then click the gear icon and select the correct microphone or audio interface. If you're using a USB microphone and you don't see it in the list, wait a while and it may appear, or simply unplug it and plug it in again.

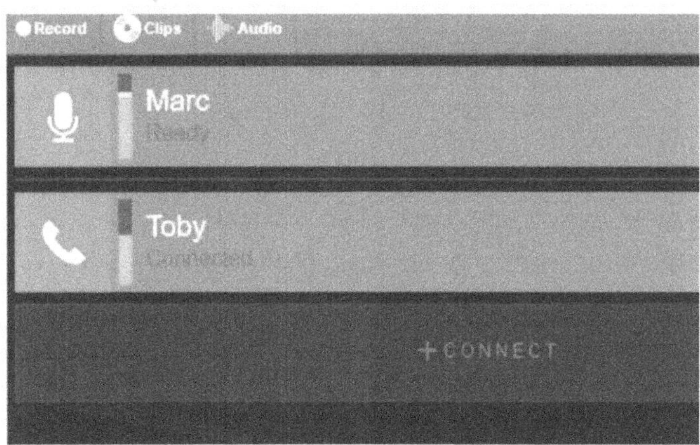

Check the levels are OK. Green is good, but try to peak in the yellow area. Any signal in the red section means that you are probably distorting. If the levels are low, try boosting the controls outside your computer before boosting inside Cleanfeed or the computer sound interface, so the volume on the interface unit or on the microphone itself. All sorted? Right, next check that you have enough hard drive or SSD space to record your interview.

Press the large +Connect button in the middle of the screen and enter the email of the guest you want to record an interview with. Then click the INVITE button. Don't worry, Cleanfeed won't store the email address, so the Prime Minister or whoever you're interviewing, won't be sent any marketing materials after your interview session! Then your guest will receive a screen like this one asking them to connect using Cleanfeed. So they just need to click CONNECT. Once connected, you'll see a new row in the main Cleanfeed studio screen with a green and white Telephone icon and the name of your guest. Your guest's audio meter will be shown on this row of the studio screen, too. Each row also functions as a button to mute, or unmute the guest when you press on it. Cool eh? Doesn't this make us podcaster's life easy?

You can repeat this process to invite additional guests to the session. You, and each of your guests, have a row in the main Cleanfeed studio screen. By the way, guests don't need a Cleanfeed account of their own, you just need one. Their CONNECT button has just one purpose — connecting them to your session.

Now that your guest is connected to the Cleanfeed session and able to chat to you, it's time to check that everyone can hear everyone else clearly. If your podcast has two presenters, and you are both using a separate computer but sat close together, separately logged into Cleanfeed to talk to the guest who is remote, you may get a nasty echo, so you really must all be wearing headphones.

Your guest should be doing this as well, and hopefully by plugging in headphones to their laptop or whatever, this will mute their loudspeaker. If you still hear echo, it is almost certainly an issue at the contributor's end. You can check this by asking your contributor to be quiet, and you speak. If you see their little audio meter moving around, you'll know that they have their speaker on at their end, which is picking up your voice on their microphone and creating a nasty echo on the output at base. So, once you've done a technical check, you should be already to go!

Now let's record the interview. Press the Record button in the top left corner of the main Cleanfeed studio screen, which will display the options available to you for the recording. Then press the orange Record button to begin the recording.

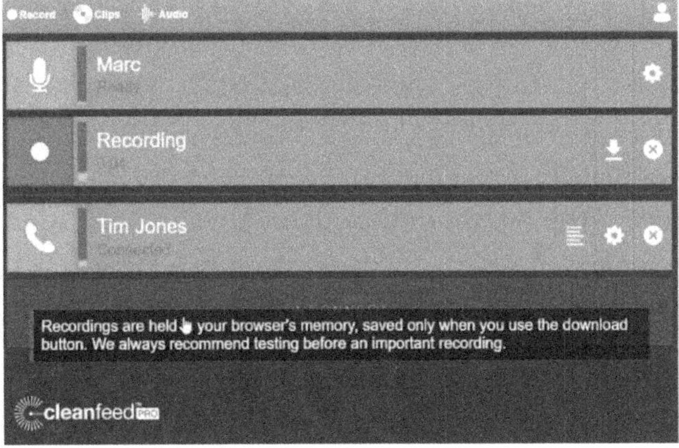

Recordings are held in your browser's memory and then you download afterwards, so always do a quick test of this before you do the main recording. The recording is shown in its own row on the screen, which also functions as a pause button, with a Record icon of a white circle in a red square. You will see the Recording meter moving up and down when you or your guests speak. Remember, you may want to mute a guest if they are not contributing at the moment to give a cleaner output to the whole podcast. When a host or guest is muted, the green icon turns dark grey, and the word Muted appears beneath their name. Press on their row to unmute them, and you'll see the icon restored to green.

Saving your recording as you go along is good practice, and most people save every 15 to 20 minutes or so.

On the right side of the Recording row, press the white Save icon , which looks like an arrow pointing downwards. Your browser will save the file to your computer.

You can now open this file in your audio editor, and check that you recorded what you meant to, by opening it all up in Audacity, Adobe Audition or your audio editor of choice. For longer recordings, you can press the Save icon at any time to save an intermediate recording, which you can do again and again. I'm a big fan of belts and braces. In fact I also record the output of the computer on a solid state recorder, just in case, but I've never needed the back up recording yet.

Now very importantly, if you forget to record the interview, or to save it properly, or you want a copy of something from ages ago that you can't find anymore, you can't just contact Cleanfeed and ask for a copy. Everything is encrypted, and nobody at the offices of Cleanfeed is listening to you, or recording anything at all. So it's totally and absolutely secure, but it also means that there is no backup copy, so make sure you test before you record.

The Pro version of Cleanfeed gives you more control of the audio, so you can start adding background music clips, recording to separate tracks so you can edit in the multitrack sections of Adobe Audition and so on, and much more.

It doesn't need a particularly fast Internet connection either, so I would recommend you look at this system. Cleanfeed has started to be used more and more to help actors, writers and theatre groups stage and produce radio dramas and plays when the pandemic hit and theatres were closed, and you can get superb audio quality even when many people are "live" at the same time.

You can get started without external mixers. The minimum requirements are just a browser and a microphone; and Cleanfeed handles the rest. You can bring together everyone on the same session. You can choose how to record them, too; even on separate tracks. What's more, with Cleanfeed Pro, with 48KHz sampling rate, you get even better cleaner sound quality and you are offered multitrack recording as well, so, for example if it's you interviewing four guests in a podcast, every track can be kept separate, and you can simply open up the multitrack file in your favourite audio editing program later to mix down. Yes, you could do everything in a Zoom type conversation, but quite often ends of words get clipped as someone else chips in with a comment. When you record every contributor cleanly, you have so much more flexibility for the mix afterwards.

Also, and you'll appreciate this if you've done a radio show, you get a virtual "cart rack". Tape cartridges used to be used in radio stations for jingles and idents, music beds, commercials and promos and so on. Cleenfeed offers a screen where you can load up your "cart rack" and play them into your podcast recording, live; a very cool feature!

Only one party needs a Cleanfeed account; just send a web link. Anyone can connect from Mac, Windows, Linux or Android.

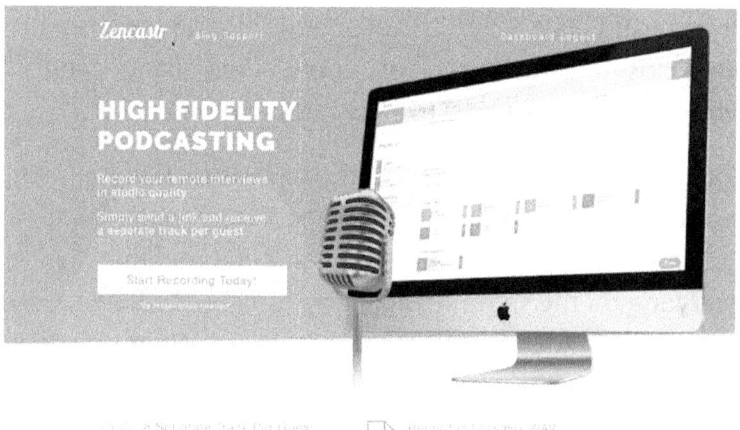

ZENCASTR

Finally, there is **Zencastr.com** which offers a similar system of providing quality audio as Cleanfeed, and an easy way of recording guests at a distance. You create an episode and send the invite link to your guest, and they accept the invite and you simply press record. Do this for every guest. Once everyone is joined to begin, each participant audio will be recorded to locally – so it should be good quality as long as their microphone and environment is good at their end, and it all gets streamed to your cloud drive, such as Dropbox.

Once the recording is finished, a separate studio quality track per guest will be automatically available in your cloud drive, along with a levelled and enhanced mix track ready for publishing. Zencastr requires no installation for you or your guests, and the audio is available immediately for editing. All that's needed is a computer, microphone and a modern browser. Clever eh?

Zencastr officially works on both Chrome and Firefox, though the company recommends using Chrome. After you finish recording your episode, it's time to work on post-processing.

Zencastr does offer a built-in processing tool and export options, but remember that Zencastr or the other two I am talking about here do not include publishing or hosting capabilities. Therefore, you need to download the final mix at some point and upload to your host.

The Automatic Postproduction button enables the Leveller that corrects volume differences between tracks and a Noise Gate which blocks background sounds during pauses. It also offers a Cross Gate - this analyses who is talking and cleverly decreases the other tracks.

Zencastr currently limits the use of its automatic postproduction to 10 hours per month. They show you your remaining allotment each time you submit a file. I personally would rather do all my post processing and cleaning up of sound in Adobe Audition or Audacity, but that's only because I know these programs well.

Zencastr offers a permanently free Hobbyist account. With this account, you can host up to two guests and can record a total of eight hours per month. For Hobbyist accounts, Zencastr records tracks as 128Kbps MP3 files and charges per use of its Automatic Postproduction option. Users who sign up for a Hobbyist account get a 14-day trial of the Professional account.

The next account tier, Professional, is a chargeable option. In addition to offering an unlimited number of guests and recordings, the Professional account level also introduces a Live Editing Soundboard, 16-bit 44.1kHz WAV recordings, and 10 hours of automatic postproduction per month.

The three systems I have mentioned here, and others with similar systems like Cast, Squadcast, Ringr, Ecamm, are so good for podcasters who need to regularly interview guests and have started to be used more and more to help actors, writers and theatre groups stage and produce radio dramas and plays especially when the pandemic hit and theatres were closed, and you can get superb audio quality even when many people are "live" at the same time in different parts of the world.

So in this section we've looked at basic recording using a computer and audio software, and also the clean feed system, which records in the cloud and gives you an awful lot of features that the podcaster needs. But there are also solutions with all-in-one devices, that are aimed for the podcaster and we'll cover those in the next section.

RECORDING – HARDWARE SOLUTIONS

If you are going to record guests in one location every week, because this could be a regular situation in an organisation, where maybe the marketing department has set up a little studio in their office, with the microphones and they just need to record it, and don't need to use something like Cleanfeed or any internet based system. There's no problem with that, and for years I have been physically travelling to various organisations to record podcasts, using my trusty portable mixer which has got 4 microphone inputs.

It's an AZDEN FMX42u, a pretty old model and I'm not even sure if they make this anymore, but you just sit this battery-operated mixer on the desk, plug in up to four clip on microphones, and the output of this mixer goes into a solid state recorder. The disadvantage of course, is that you have to do your mixing on the fly, and so you don't have the opportunity of keeping four separate channels afterwards for mixing. But for quickly recording multiple people, a system like this still works fine for me!

But technology has really moved on...check out the following devices!

If you really want to do the physical recordings, you may like to invest in the nifty Zoom PodTrak P4 Podcasting device. The main machine is battery operated, with a mains adapter, and has four XLR inputs and low noise preamps. You can plug in limiters to each microphone, to stop any distortion if things get rowdy during your recording, and there is a low-cut filter as well to get rid of any buzz or hum in the location where you're recording.

The ZOOM podcasting <u>bundle</u> comes with headphones which have individual volume controls and microphones and stands and is a complete package for about $750.00. It comes with buttons or pads as they call them, that can trigger your intro and outro jingles, commercials, and even has built in sound effects that you may want! You can record interviews on the phone as well by connecting your smartphone via special cable that plugs in the side of the device. Or you may want to use Bluetooth.

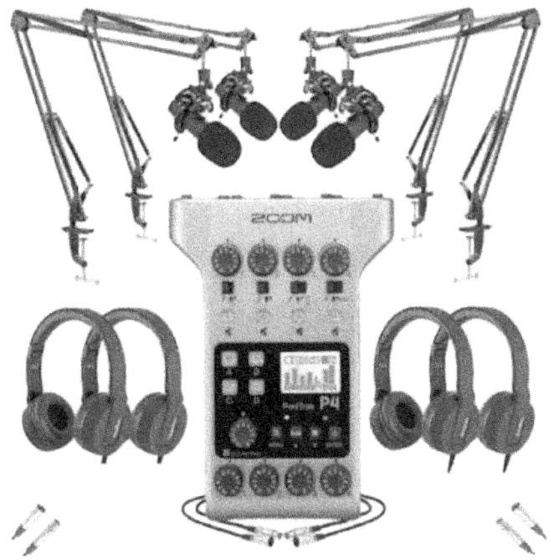

You can record your podcast on your Zoom P4 device on an internal SD card, and afterwards you can transfer the data to your computer, and get a 10 channel multitrack, in other words every separate channel, plus the sound effects as well, and the interview channel, so you can get the levels just right. Or go for a live podcast if you wish, it's up to you!

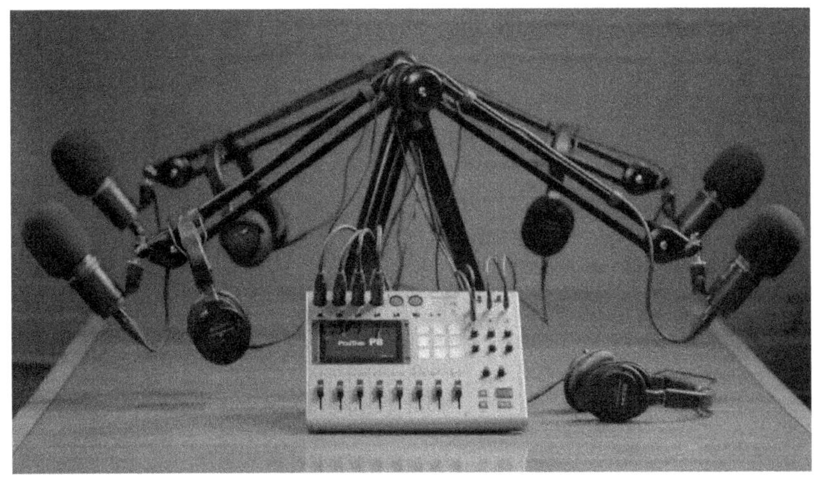

A device that's bigger from Zoom and is much more ergonomic is their P8, also available as a bundle with microphone and headphones if you want them, or you can just buy the device on its own. This is very user friendly and less fiddly than the P4, and has 6 microphone inputs. Everything is colour coded so it's easy to wire up. The Zoom PodTrak P8 is an all-in-one recording, editing and mixing solution with cool touchscreen controls and like the P4 has, with pre-loaded sounds like applause, laughter and so on and you can of course load your own sounds for playing in live.

Like the P4, you get a dedicated channel where you can record phone calls so you can incorporate guests into your show. It also features onboard editing options so you can trim, split and fade audio clips to create a polished finished product.

Finally, how about the Rodecaster Pro?

The RØDECaster™ Pro offers 4 microphone channels that are able to power studio condenser microphones with the 48 volt "phantom power" as well as conventional dynamic microphones. You can quickly connect microphones for you and your guests with automatic level setting and one-touch recording to a microSD card. The RØDECaster Pro comes with eight programmable sound effects pads, for instant triggering of sound effects, music, jingles, applause and ads. You can record audio direct to the programmable pads from any input, or simply "drag and drop" files from your computer using the supplied software. You can even select your favourite colours for the pad illumination.

What about remote interviews? You connect your smartphone to the RØDECaster Pro via Bluetooth™ or with a 4-pin TRRS cable. Like the Zoom machines, the device automatically provides "mix-minus" audio to prevent echo being heard by the caller.

The RØDECaster Pro's pristine preamps and outputs feature Class A circuitry, as found in broadcast consoles. The Class A preamps provide a much cleaner gain structure with lower levels of distortion. The result is an incredibly clean, low-noise signal. The Preamps are also servo-biased, keeping distortion levels low. The RØDECaster Pro also features multistage dynamics, such as compression, limiting, de-essing and noise-gating.

The RØDECaster Pro operates as a standalone unit straight out of the box, recording your finished podcast direct to a microSD™ card. It also connects to your computer as a USB audio interface, so you can record your podcast to your audio recording software, or you can stream live. And you can record in multi-channel mode, allowing you to separately record each of the sources to its own track for later post-production.

These all-in-one hardware solutions are amazing for podcast production, but they really are only for that. If you are thinking that you might branch out into other type of production work, such as voice over, radio drama, or music production, you may be better off with recording and editing the traditional way and learning a fully featured software programme like Adobe Audition or Audacity, as that will give you much more flexibility and scalability.

But if your podcast is going to be based in one location, where you have regular guests physically with you, with people to be interviewed externally just now and again, then look at one of the all-in-one units I've showed you in this section, they could be just right for you. Don't forget if you are doing this as a business or part of a business activity, you can claim back the costs of this gear back off your tax in most countries. Ask your accountant for details.

SETTING UP YOUR HOME PODCAST STUDIO

So, can you set up your home podcast studio on a limited budget? I am well aware that you may not have the resources to afford to build a broadcast quality recording studio with top-end equipment at home to record your podcasts.

I'll assume that cash is tight, but the good news is that you don't have to make your studio pretty, it's only the sound that you need to worry about. You need to find a good place in your home where you can set up your microphone or microphones if you are going to have studio co-presenters or guests.

What does a good recording location need to be? It's two things:

1 - **Somewhere very quiet, with a low "noise floor".**

2 – **Somewhere that is acoustically very "dead" with minimal sound reflections giving "echo" or reverberations.**

First, I'll explain what a noise floor is. Basically, a noise floor is the level that you get on the recording software meter when you are not saying anything, and breathing very quietly. Some people call this "room noise", and the noise floor is measured in decibels. And the lower the noise floor is, the better it is. You may think this is going to go into geek territory, and it's not that important, but you want to sound professional, don't you? It's so annoying for listeners when they have noises in the background, and it sounds like you're recording the podcast in a tunnel or something which is extremely frustrating. Also, you may also want to record more than podcasts in there, and move into recording audio books, or proper voiceover work or voice acting work for animations or video games. There you really will have to have high technical standards, or your work will be rejected.

It's generally considered that minus 60 decibels is a good noise floor, and if you measure anything quieter than minus 60 decibels, that is pretty good. Once you've calibrated your recording software so it records your voice at a decent level, not too soft so it creates background hiss, and not so loud that it is distorted, then stop talking and see what the room noise is. On your software audio meter, you will see in decibels what that noise floor is. And if it's lower than minus 60 decibels, you are in a good situation.

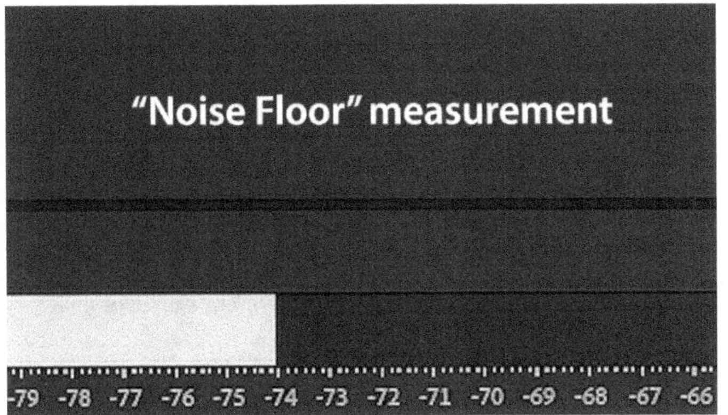

But what about the room echo? If you clap your hands in the area you want to record in, and it sounds "live", like you can hear the clap reverberates around, that's not good.

Ideally you should be in an area surrounded by soft furnishings, curtains and drapes, cushions. If you have a big enough bedroom, then try and put your recording area in that. Make a sort of tunnel affair out of old duvets and blankets, and then put a desk in there, covered with a blanket as well, and put your microphones and laptop in there as well. If you can afford it, check out acoustic blankets, and make frames that can hang these really heavy sound- absorbing blankets around the area where you are going to record, or you could hang them from hooks in the ceiling.

Remember, it's audio!

It doesn't have to LOOK pretty!

Essentially, you want to form a sort of "dead room" around your recording area. As you start to convert your recording area, clap your hands to see how you're getting on. If you can't hear any reverberation at all, like you were in the middle of a field outside, then you are doing a good job. This means that your podcast will sound professional, and not amateurish with lots of nasty reverb and echo ruining your acoustics.

By the way, when it comes to laptops, I hope you have got a quiet one! If you have got an old fashioned one with a hard drive that whizzes round, and also gets hot so it has a loud fan, maybe it's time to trade it in for a new laptop with a solid state drive, or SSD, that is completely silent, with no fans at all.

You'll most likely be reading scripts off your laptop which will be right near your microphone, so it's important for this to be quiet. Of course, you could have an iPad or another tablet which is also silent, or good old-fashioned paper, as long as you don't rustle it too much!

Once you've set up your table, where you are going to record your podcast, cover the table with a blanket, or some kind of material, you need to make sure that you are surrounded by things that can absorb sound no that will reflect sound. Keep in mind that you may have a live guest or a co presenter so leave space for them as well. But don't leave too much space.

You may want to follow social distancing, but from an audio point of view, remember that if you have two or more microphones open in one room, it's going to be difficult to get a nice close miked sound for everybody, but that's not a problem if you are recording separate channels, and then you can select the person who is speaking only when you are in edit later.

So what equipment will you need as a very basic list?

You'll need:

> **A good quality microphone & a plosive pop filter**
>
> **A microphone stand**
>
> **A computer interface box if you have analogue microphones**
>
> **A computer**
>
> **Quality screened cables**
>
> **and Audio editing software.**

Let's go through these items one by one. The first thing that people get excited about is the microphone, and this is a very personal choice, but basically you need to pay as much as you can really afford, especially if you are thinking of getting into the world of professional voice over work as well as podcast production.

These days, there are so many excellent microphones around, and in a way it's a bit like cars in that it's not like the old days when there were some terrible cars around. There are very few terrible microphones around these days, as technology has advanced so much. But I need to tell you that there are two types of microphones.

There are USB microphones, and these simply plug into a USB socket of a computer, and the computer should recognise the microphone immediately and record on your software as long as that microphone is selected. The other type of microphone is an analogue microphone, which in its semi-professional , or professional form has a socket called an XLR connection.

It's called this because there are three wires connected to the plugs and socket. The "X" is the earth, The "L" pin carries the left signal, and the "R" pin carries the right signal. Now there are various advantages and disadvantages of the two types of microphone. The USB microphone sounds cool because you can plug it straight into your computer.

However, you will not be able to plug it into an audio mixer or a solid-state audio recorder, and so it won't give you that much flexibility in your studio. The analogue microphone that have an XLR socket, can plug into a wide variety of other machines. However, if you want to connect an analogue microphone to a digital computer, and yes, all computers are digital, I've yet to find an analogue computer(!) You'll need an interface box. There are lots of USB interface boxes around - I would recommend the Focusrite Solo Scarlett box which is great quality and not expensive, and you simply plug your microphone in there into the XLR socket, and then the Focusrite Solo Scarlett box connects by a USB socket into your computer.

There is a headphone socket on the box, and also it has a 48 Volt power switch. All professional microphones and most semi-professional microphones need what is called "Phantom power "of 48 volts, so the little Focusrite Scarlett box can provide this. If it's not switched on, the microphone simply won't work! By the way, if you are going to have regular co presenters physically with you, you need to get the Focusrite interface box that has two or more inputs not just one as the Solo model has.

I won't go through all the various microphones out there, because I don't want to confuse you with a lot of technical stuff, and there are plenty of websites that can give you more information if you want, but if you're looking for a really good quality microphone for about $125 or equivalent currency, you can't go wrong with an Audio Technica ATR 2500 microphone, which is a USB microphone, and my choice for a quality budget analogue microphone with an XLR socket, is the AKG P120 or one of it's bigger brothers that come with a useful shock reducing cradle.

Don't forget when you're looking for a good microphone to look at the second-hand market.   You may find a fantastic bargain by looking at eBay or equipment gear websites selling second hand audio equipment. If you find, for example, a Neumann TLM 103 microphone for $300 or so, snap it up, As brand new they are more than double this. As long as the microphone has been cared for, and not dropped at all, it should be absolutely fine.

As well as a microphone, you need something to put it in. Some microphones come with a cradle which protects the microphone from vibrations. If your microphone doesn't come with one, you can buy third party microphone cradles. They are important, especially if you are going to be working from a desk, and vibrations from your hand and arm on the desk may be picked up by the microphone.

When it comes to a microphone stand, avoid the tabletop ones, and go for a boom arm, the ones that musicians have, because there again there is no contact with the desk in front of you.

With all microphones, to be able to get close to them to speak into them, you need to buy a separate "pop filter". These are made of fine gauze, and stop the plosive sounds like on the letter "p" creating nasty overloads on the audio signal. So basically, you hide your microphone behind the pop filter, and you talk into the actual pop filter! We recommend that you buy the best quality filter you can, ideally a double one. These things look like their muffling your voice, but they should be completely acoustically transparent.

Right, let's talk cables. Don't skimp on the quality of the cable, because your cables can easily pick up mains hum, that can completely ruin a podcast. So make sure you buy good quality screened cable, that is nice and thick, and ideally has gold contacts on the plugs and sockets so they'll offer better connections and won't tarnish over time.

If you are always going to have studio guests and co presenters, consider getting yourself a little audio mixer. We looked at all-in-one podcast solutions earlier, but maybe you don't need anything as sophisticated if you're using a basic computer and software setup. A 6 channel mixer like a Soundcraft EPM 6 would be absolutely fine for your needs, and you'll be able to scale up to do all sorts of other things with a mixer like that.

You could run the mixer like a radio station does, if you're recording everything as live, and put up contributors faders as and when. If you have every microphone open at once, it will sound awful, so if you know that you are about to interview someone, your guest microphone can be slid up on the mixer, and taken down when they have finished.

The other advantage of using a mixer, is that you can record a standby copy of everything, on a solid-state recorder as I mentioned before. It would be awful to finish what you thought was a recording, but something went wrong and you have a distorted file or there's simply nothing there. So one output of the mixer could go into a solid state recorder as a backup which just records everything as you do your podcast, and another output of your mixer could then go via the digital interface into your computer for editing later.

I would make sure that the solid state recorder is set to a level a little bit below that of the computer input, just in case things gets a little bit heated or noisy during the podcast recording. Having a backup on your solid-state recorder, will be slightly lower level, and hopefully will not record the distortion you got on the computer.

So what kind of computer do you need? Most modern-day computers will be fine for audio, it's not as if you are doing any high-end production, a modern Mac or Windows computer will be able to record and edit audio for the needs of an average podcast, but look for at least 8 GB of RAM.   As mentioned before, I would recommend 3 software programmes to you - the paid one is Adobe Audition, which is really a professional software programme with many features, including an excellent multitrack interface, and lots of noise reduction capabilities. But in a very close second is Audible, which is astonishingly free, although I do suggest that you donate to the developers of this excellent audio programme. Then there's the highly featured NCH Wavepad software program which is free for personal use but very inexpensive for professional use.

In these software programmes, you'll be able to move content around, and insert features, jingles, and so on. Audio software programmes also offer many features, and I'll just quickly talk about equalisation, and compression.

Equalisation or as we call it in the audio world "EQ" , is a way of fixing poorly recorded audio. For example, if you do find there is a nasty hum all the way through your recording, or you do hear traffic rumble or whatever, EQ can help make the sound better. on your software, you will find there are two types of equalisation. There's parametric, and a graphic equaliser. A graphic equaliser is the easiest to understand to begin with.

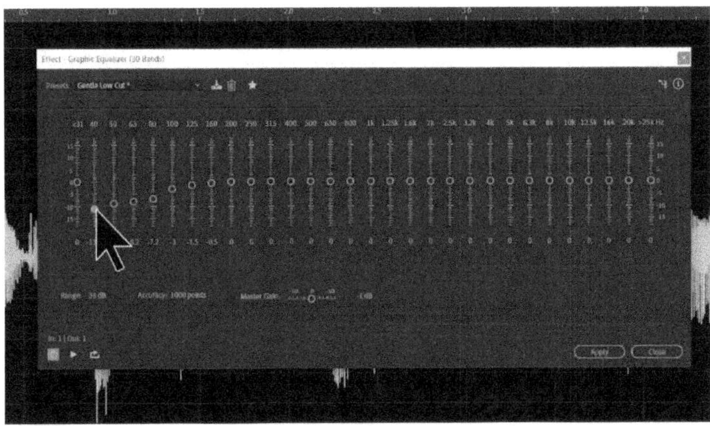

Here you'll see all the frequencies from the lowest on the left right the way up to the highest, even higher than a human can hear. For example, if you wanted to reduce the frequencies around 50 or 60 Hertz, to reduce mains hum, this is the fader that you pull down, and you would play around with the faders to adjust. But of course, doing this may also get rid of the nice bass sound of your presenter's voice! So that's why it's important to record cleanly in the 1st place, and not rely on software to try and fix problems in edit.

The other feature that software programmes offer is called compression. That means that all the low and high-volume peaks and troughs are all crushed down, and that makes a much more consistent volume level throughout your podcast, and it makes it easier for people to hear.

You don't want to overdo the compression, or else it will sound like one of those annoying 1990's dance tracks, which are very hard to listen to, but most radio stations apart from classical music ones compress their output, because it makes listening easier, especially when there is background noise, for example listening in a car, or in a noisy gym.

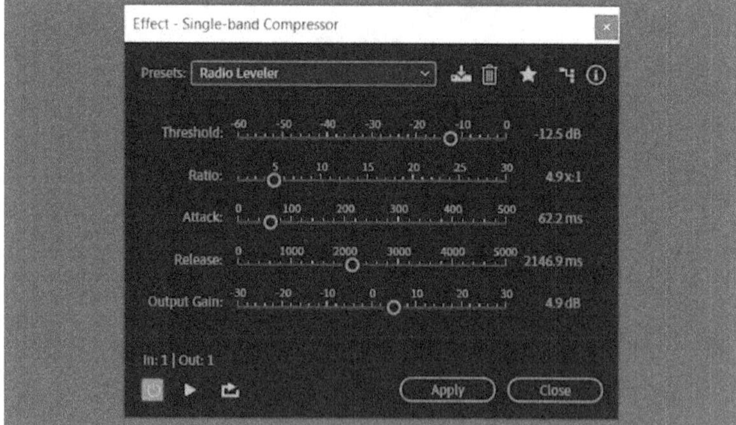

Inside the settings of your compressor, whether it's a hardware box, or in your software, you may see Threshold. This knob determines how loud the audio has to get before the compressor starts working. If you set the threshold to the very quietest parts of your audio, anything louder than the quietest parts will be compressed. So you need to experiment with this. You may also have a setting called Noise Floor so you can make sure that any silence isn't amplified during pauses in you talking. And Ratio will determine the level of compression.

3:1 compression ratio is sort of light compression, and 6:1 is heavy compression, but you need to use your ears, forget what it says on the software controls! You will also find attack and delay settings which adjust the reaction speed of the compressor.

If you're not technical at all, you don't have to worry too much about the equalisation or compression, your main aim, is to record voices cleanly, in a good location, so you don't have to play around too much with the sound afterwards to fix anything.

TECHNICAL CONSIDERATIONS – THE BASICS

In this section I'm going to go through the basic technical considerations and some top tips for recording quality audio, so you may want to skip this if you already know about recording, and you may even be a voice over or studio manager who simply wants to know how to get into the world of podcast. So you may be excused this section!

Now, you may say to me, *"I'm making a podcast, aimed at people who are really into the subject matter, and desperate to hear my content. It's not going to a fussy broadcaster or audiobook company with their strict technical rules who may reject my uploads; why does good audio quality matter?"*   Well, it's true that as I'm sure you will appreciate, even national broadcasters have had to put up with putting out interviews with people with a terrible technical quality, simply because the pandemic has meant that they had to do interviews via phones, or Zoom or whatever. But, if you really want to get a good impression, and create a podcast, that simply sounds professional, please follow the tips that I'll be giving you here, as it doesn't cost a fortune in equipment or extra time in recording and edit to achieve high audio standards. And you WILL lose fans if you constantly create audio with distortion, hiss or hum in the background or if there is constant echo on your interview recordings.....and it's a fallacy that Apple Podcast for example will accept any old quality, as they won't!

You see, at the end of the day, people have become fussier over the quality of their audio. Back in the days of transistor radios and black and white television sets, we were grateful for anything that we had in the home that could relay to us what was going on in the world, but these days many of us love to have a large screen 4K or high definition television set with HiFi soundbars and subwoofers, and more large homes have a separate room for a "Home Cinema" where good sound quality is paramount, so if your podcast comes across as distorted, full of background hiss, echoes and distracting sounds, it's not going to be an easy listen is it, even if the editorial content is gripping? If you are producing a podcast for your company or another organisation, you need to reflect the professionalism of the business and corporate world. You may think that you need to have really high end equipment to be able to come up with audio that is of the quality of a broadcaster, such as the BBC, but that's not the case at all these days. Solid state digital equipment is so incredibly inexpensive, so that's not an excuse anymore!

However you could be the type of person who is not that technical at all, and that's fine, we can't all be good at everything, and in fact you may want to editorially produce your podcast, but have nothing to do with the technical side at all, and you're happy to outsource the whole technical side to either a voice over artist who has his or her own studio who will record and edit your podcast together for you or you could use a podcast production company, who specialise in podcast production, or you could be more in control by using one of the services that automatically do the technical stuff for you after you have recorded it.

 So for example, you could interview people and keep the recordings and your own introductions and links as separate files then upload them to a site which offers a service where you assemble it on the site and they make it much easier than having to learn an audio software program. There are two main ones that I recommend; one is called www.Alitu.com and the other one is www.Spreaker.com .

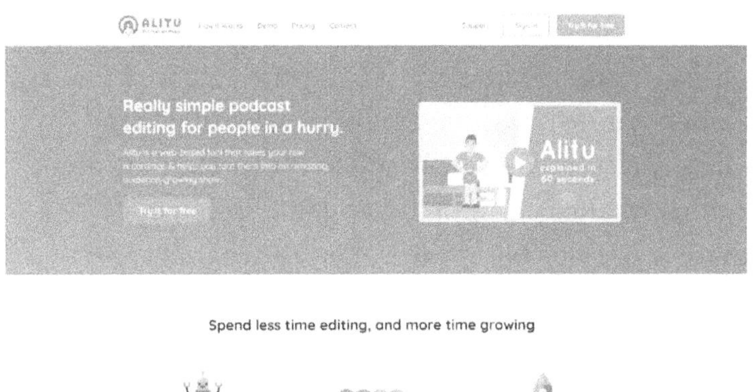

Spend less time editing, and more time growing

The way these sites work is that you can upload your raw files, and the clever software automatically optimises the sound levels, does its best to improve the sound quality as well if it has been recorded in a noisy place, and then intelligently splits up the files so you have the choice as to what order to put things in. You then put the blocks in order and works out the timings, and it's all pretty clever.

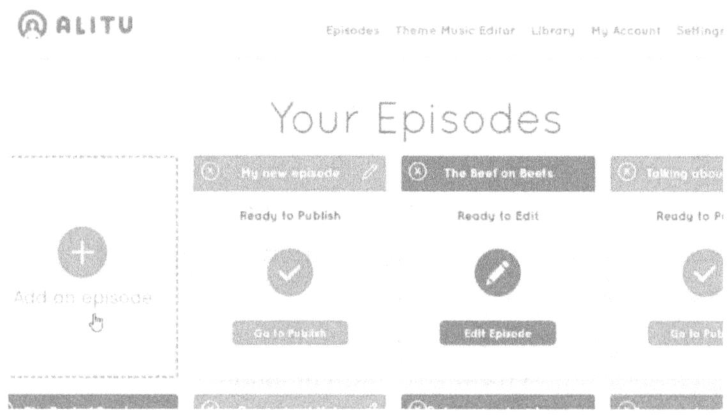

You're welcome to try these systems out, but you do have to pay for them, and you may want to be more in control by learning the basics of audio software programs like Audacity or Adobe Audition.   So, even if you think you are technophobic, I suggest you take my suggestions for learning the software which isn't that complicated, and I will show you how to optimise your audio and edit using both Audacity which is a free software programme that you can download, and also Adobe Audition which is high end audio editing software.

If I could give you a list of the very basics that your technical considerations have to cover, it would be that every speaker in your podcast would be close to their microphone, but not so close that it would create nasty peaks or plosives that again sound unprofessional. You would make every speaker in your podcast clear to listen to free from distortion such as clipping or interference or simply touching or handling the microphone. And you must make sure that the volume levels are consistent throughout, so that the listener isn't turning up or down their volume control as they listen through.

A lot of this can be done by making sure that you record in the same place for every podcast, whether this is an office that has been kitted out for podcast recording, or a place in your home which you can call your podcast studio. The next section I'll go through where in the home would be the best place to reduce acoustic reflections and thus reduce any echo, and to make it sound really good, but it's so important to start with the basic principles rather than record whatever you can, and then spend ages trying to save the audio to improve it in your software later.

 If you record very clean and clear audio to begin with, it makes your life so much easier later in edit, even though, as well see, software these days, even the free ones, come with pretty good noise reduction features.

Recording audio successfully, so it sounds clean, undistorted and without background hiss, comes down to using decent equipment and wires as well as choosing a good recording environment, but don't forget technique! For example, remembering not ever touching the microphone when you are recording. Use a really decent microphone boom pole on a stand, or if you really have to a desk holder, although desk microphone holders tend to pick up vibrations so watch out for that.

Good technique also means keeping the same distance between you and the microphone. Usually there should be about 3 to 4 inches from your mouth to the essential double pop filter, and then another three to four inches to the centre of the microphone .

Also watch for cables used for microphones that are next to mains cables that could easily pick up nasty hum. As with most things in life, the weak link of any chain will determine the output quality. So if you've got an expensive microphone, but a very cheap and dodgy mixer with crackly output, well you know that's not going to be good news.

INTROS, LINERS, SPONSOR BUMPERS AND OUTROS

You can just start and end your podcast with you or your colleagues talking, there's no law about having to have some kind of musical introduction and ending to your podcast, but it's kind of traditional, and it can give a nice professional touch to your show.

As well as giving a nice start to a show, an introduction with a small piece of music, is kind of an "ear worm " do help people remember your podcast. It's like the signature tunes of radio DJ's of retro radio! It's up to you what you want, but if I was giving my suggestions to you, all I would say is don't make it too long, and don't over promise and under deliver. In other words, don't have a fantastic big build-up, with an "all-singing all-dancing" introduction, and then the rest of the show goes rather flat. A podcast intro doesn't even need to be up-tempo, it just needs to be in tune with the feel of the podcast.

So where can you get podcast jingles from? If it's just a very simple small bed of music, and a voice over, you might like to just get a voice over artist to send you some recordings, that you would mix yourself; see the MULTITRACK section for details. But if you do feel like outsourcing it to someone who has some more *whistles and bells* at their command, you really can't do better than to go to the **fiverr.com** site.

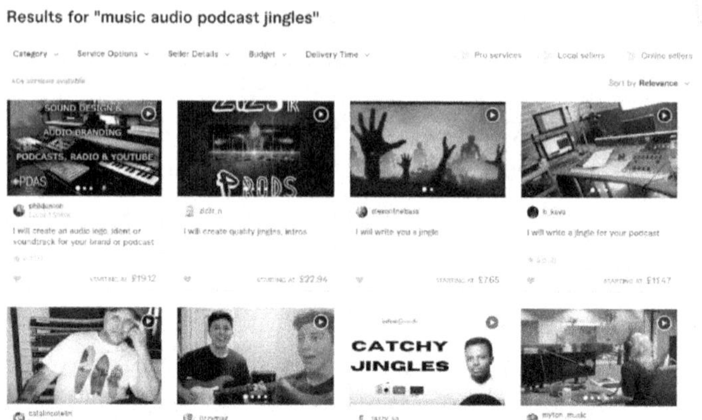

Just search **music audio podcast jingles** on the Fiverr.com site, and you will find many suppliers, who have their own music studios at home, and can create for you a customised music intro, even sung jingles, with block harmonies and all, for extremely reasonable fees.

So what do you need? An intro of about 10 to 15 seconds maximum, and an outro of about the same duration. You might like to consider an intro that leads into a soft music bed, or it doesn't have to be soft, but make sure that the level of the music is under your voice, so that your introduction or menu, isn't drowned by the music.

Sometimes it's nice to have an introduction to a podcast with some music underneath you, and then it fades out after the introduction and then the rest of the podcast you don't need music behind it, in fact I would actively say don't have it. Other inserts you might like to consider would be jingles for any features you have, and these again can be simple voice over or someone's if you like, you might like to have something very retro, or cheesy, or just keep it plain.

When you start to get some advertisers or sponsors on board, they would appreciate some professional production as well, so again you can get a supplier on a site like Fiverr, to create a radio advert or a sponsor bumper, that you can play in to your podcast how many times you have agreed with the advertiser or sponsor.

A word of warning when it comes to music, and that is you must avoid all copyright music. In other words, released pop or rock music, commercially released music of any kind. There are plenty of copyright free music libraries out there, and they are very flexible with styles of music, and edit points, so check them out. **Soundstripe.com** and **epidemicsound.com** both have specific categories for podcasts and podcast jingles.

You may have a podcast about music, and you want to play clips, you may have a film review podcast, and he want to play excepts, that has music in, that's fine if you get permission from the Copyright Holder, otherwise the podcast directory, will sniff out that you have Copyright music on your podcast, and will most probably ask you to edit those sections out.

THE MAIN PODCAST RECORDING SESSION

When it comes to the recording day, and you and maybe your co presenter are all set up and ready, record just the introduction, and then stop and play it back. Just check that everything is all okay technically. If, when you play it back on the big speakers, you may suddenly realise you hear something you did not hear in your headphones, such as mains hum, or that you left another microphone open that is plugged into the mixer, or something like that.

It's always worth doing a technical check, as all professional radio presenters do, and they check the equipment before they go live on air. It's like a comprehensive check that pilots do before they take off to an aircraft. Yes, it's amazing what software can do to improve sound, but why spend a lot of time and effort trying to fix sound afterwards, when it can be recorded superbly in the 1st place, just by checking the first few minutes?

As well as a technical check, make sure that you as the presenter, and any co presenters, are in the right frame of mind. This is something else that broadcasters have to cope with, and if your " on air radio personality" is of a "happy go lucky" cheerful voice, and you've just had a terrible morning, and just been told bad news, and you've got a toothache, well, it doesn't matter! The show must go on! So, like the best actors, you are a show person as well behind the microphone, and so no matter how you feel, you must give a consistent performance, and portray a consistent personality to your previous episodes of the podcast.

Give yourself a few minutes to actively think of this before you push the record button, just settle yourself down, and maybe even listen to the last podcast you did, to remind yourself of how you sounded, and boost your confidence by listing to the bits you were particularly proud of. It's amazing how powerful this is, especially when you're first starting out, when maybe your confidence isn't as strong as it should be.

But here's a warning that if there are two or three of you all co presenting, make sure you don't go down the path of just joking amongst each other, and it takes a while to actually get to any content!

I'm sure a bit of what has happened in your day so far is of interest, you don't want to be fully lacking in personality, but make sure that you are not annoying the audience by talking about irrelevancies, when listeners just want you to get on with what they have clicked on your podcast to enjoy! It's a very fine line between being a real person with real problems, that people can relate to, to being downright annoying to some listeners!

Also if you are talking to your co-presenter, don't talk over them, or shout louder and louder, because not only will this cause distortion, but it is also another source of frustration for listeners, as they can't really hear who is talking. So give the other person the curtesy of some space to say what they want before you come in with what you want to say. Good radio presenters who are working physically together in the same studio, often have a secret code when they have finished speaking, or when they have something to say.

When I worked in radio, my co-presenter always used to throw a pretend ball to me when they had finished saying everything they wanted to say, as if they were literally throwing the conch to me to continue the conversation. I did the same to them. That seemed to work very well, because to the listeners it was a seamless experience, it was very slick, there weren't any gaps, and we rarely spoke over each other. So try that and see if that works with your co presenter and yourself.   The system of throwing the imaginary ball to the other presenter when people can't see you, is also useful if you are an expert or someone who has been asked to explain something, but you've come to the end of what you want to explain, and you are getting yourself in dodgy ground, so you want your co-presenter to pick up, rather than let you flounder into an area that you don't know much about!

So what if your co presenter is talking and talking, without leaving gaps, and you desperately have something to say on that subject? Well, what you do then, is similar to what you did in class at school. You would simply put your hand up! If you're not adjusting the audio levels, then alternatively, you can look at the other presenter with big eyes, and they usually get the message to let you have a speak!

Finally, here are some quick tips for you . I'm sure that during the podcast you will be referring a lot to websites that you found or interesting pages of material, and it's so difficult to actually speak out the long web address, the URL, especially when it's not just the main website you're referring to but a page that's very difficult to find.

So if you know you're going to refer to an article or a certain sub webpage, before the recording shorten the link by using TinyURL , Pretty Links or another service, so any long and complicated URL is easy to actually say, as well as being easy for the listener to remember!

MASTERING AND EXPORTING THE mp3 WITH METADATA

So you finished your editing and it's now time to master your file. One look at the waveform should tell you if it needs major levelling work.

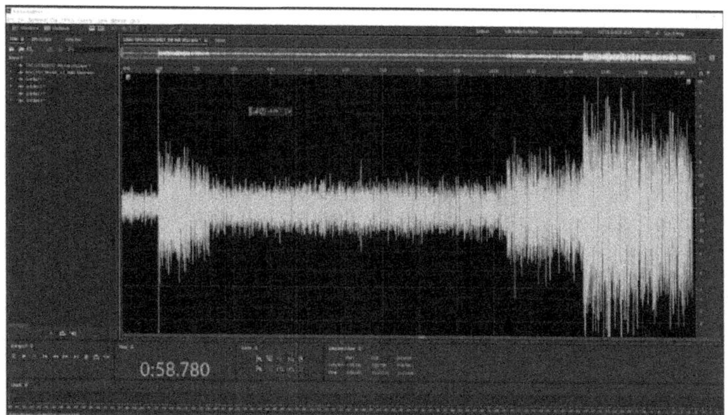

For example, this particular waveform has got some very quiet sections in and some loud ones but they are quite easy to fix, we simply highlight the quiet ones an normalise to minus 3dB. We do the same to the "loud stuff" and then everything becomes normalised to minus 3 decibels.

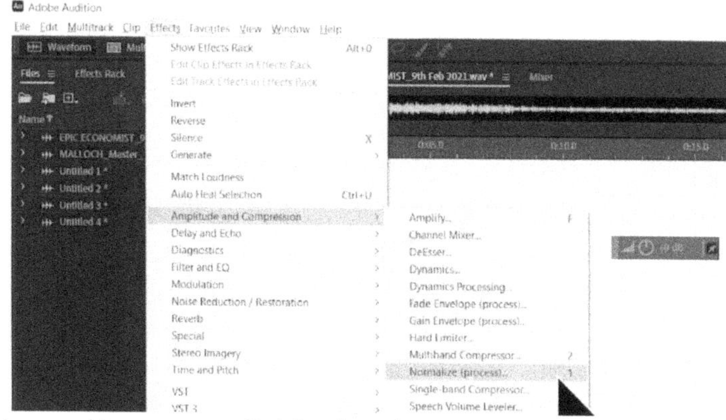

We need to save our finished podcast as MP3 files, at a data rate of 128 kilobytes per second. The maximum size of your exported file is 150 megabytes , or else it will be rejected. But don't worry - this is 2 hours and 30 seconds at that data rate, so I'm sure your podcast won't be that long! Before we export the file, we need to click on the metadata window and this is where we insert the metadata that we can "cook into" the mp3 file..

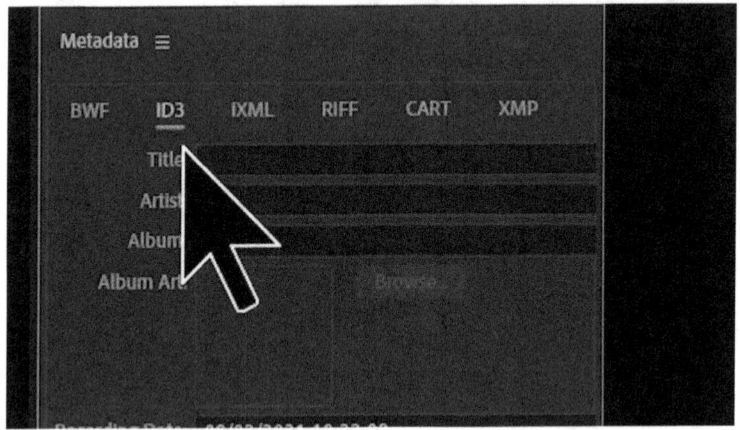

Your RSS feed that you'll send to the directories contains all your podcast metadata. This information determines what listeners see about your podcast — including the podcast cover art, episode title and descriptions.

Each metadata field is defined in different tags – some of which can be "cooked in" to your mp3 file as ID3 tags, and some are included on the RSS feed from the information you type in on the host platform before you upload it.

These tags are there to help filter through all the other podcasts that people don't want to find yours that they DO want to hear. They make our podcast files searchable and the better we add them – the easier it will be for our potential listeners to find us. You might not realize that small errors in metadata could keep your podcast off the radar of your potential listeners and that would be a real shame.

You may think this is such a big pain to fill all these in correctly and to follow the rules, but at the end of the day, just be grateful that the world of podcasting is still generally unregulated, and we are not under the same strict regulations that broadcasters are under. You should see the forms THEY have to fill in! So a little red tape is something we will have to put up with, especially if you want to grow your audience and be seen as a professional podcast producer.

You need – at least - to have these two pieces of metadata encoded WITH your mp3 file:

– Title (this is individual episode title, but not the episode number, remember people won't be searching for episode numbers).

Many podcast hosting services automatically keep track of your episodes and number them for you, it's always handy for listeners to have an episode number to refer back to. Be sensible here - if you include a long list of carefully researched keywords in an attempt to win podcast searches, your show may well be removed from the Apple directory.

It's important to have a clear, concise name for your podcast. Make your title specific.

 A show titled "Local News" or "My 2 cents" is too vague to attract many subscribers, no matter how excellent the content.

– Comments/Description (this is your short episode summary – in Apple podcast, you only see the first 100 characters, so make sure those are important ones! In some other directory's, such as Stitcher, you don't see anything unless you click the link to find out more about your podcast. The maximum amount of text allowed for this tag is 4000 characters.

Now the next pieces of meta data can be cooked into your MP3 when you save it in your software programme, but maybe this information is already in your podcast host when you fill out the form there. It may also be set up inside Podcast Connect the Apple system.

But you might as well fill it in to make sure that the MP3 file has all this information attached:

– Artist (usually a name of your podcast host).
– Album (your podcast name).
– Composer (podcast host or a production company).
– Orig. Artist (podcast host or organisation).
PLUS… – Artwork/Pictures
The artwork is a 3000 x 3000 pixel, 72 dpi jpeg or png RGB file. It's so important that it's bold, relevant and enticing! Make sure your design is effective at both its original size and at tiny thumbnail size. You must include a show title and brand as part of your podcast artwork.
– Track number – this is where you put your episode number.
– URL – this is the URL of your podcast main website, but most directories don't actually use or need this.

– Year – very important when people are looking for up to date information.

– Genre Choose "Speech" or "Comedy" if you're choosing this in the Metadata fields of your audio software, as the rest of the choices in your software export metadata tags are all related to music. This may be overridden by the podcast category anyway to be honest.

– Copyright, this is if you've used and got permission from any copyright content. If not, you own the copyright, so your name goes here.

That's all you can include with the actual file, but of course you'll find much more detailed information needed when applying to be on the Apple Podcasts directory like Language – don't ignore this and assume "it's obvious" you're English. Also don't forget to click the "explicit" button if it really is wild and late night, or else the podcast will get rejected as well! . Also, on your host website, don't leave the form fields as "default". In other words when you're filling in the form on your host website, don't just leave the "insert your name here" that has been typed in already, and think you'll get away with that, because you won't, and your podcast will get rejected.

PODCAST COVER ART

Another thing that you must put a lot of effort into when you are launching a podcast is to have an attractive looking thumbnail or as it's often called in our world of Podcast "Cover Art" . Even though the end product is an audio medium, and all of us are fans of audio, you know yourself, that when you are flicking through a long list of podcasts, you may be interested to listen to, you are going to be attracted to a powerful picture aren't you?

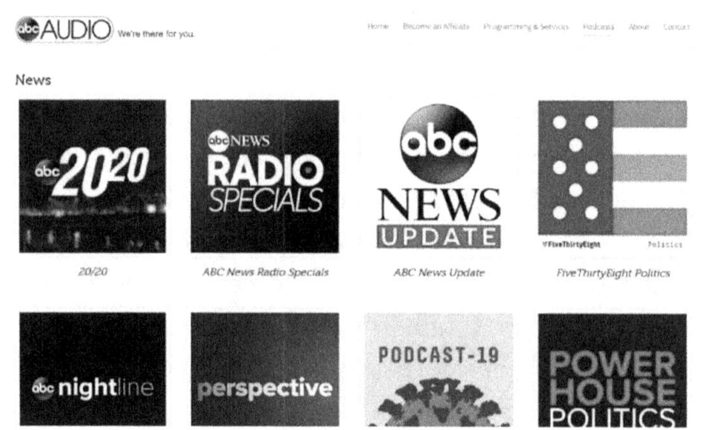

So the artwork is extremely important. Look to your competitors in your podcast genre to see what they are doing, and don't try and copy some of the best-known ones, but do something completely different, but still powerful. If you or your co presenter has an intriguing or attractive face, consider using that as part of the design, but there's no problem if you don't want your face to appear on your thumbnail!

There are plenty of ways of getting the feel for what your podcast is about with a graphic, a certain font, and you can get inspiration from looking at other podcast cover arts. The cover art is what helps listeners visually identify your podcast, and it should help your show attract new listeners and potentially gain new subscribers.

On your artwork, you must include your podcast title, and clear large fonts and relevant pictures have to be used, or if you go down any weird surreal route, it may get rejected by the good people at Apple, and other platforms. Try and go for an attractive choice of fonts, and colours with good contrast. The size needs to be square, and if you are starting from scratch, on a programme like Photoshop or Illustrator , start with an image file of 3000 by 3000 pixels. It must be in the RGB colour space, in other words an image for a screen, as against the CMYK colour space, which is for physical printing. The resolution should be 72 dots per inch and you need to save your final artwork as a JPEG or PNG file.

You'll get your artwork rejected, if anything is stolen from a copyright picture, or if anything is blurry or pixelated. You can't put any logos on there, for example from Apple, or even any visual representation of Apple hardware, which would imply it was an official podcast from Apple.

If your podcast is sponsored by someone, sorry you can't have their logo on the artwork either. You obviously can't have any explicit language, all references to drugs, violence, and no profanity of any kind at all.   But I'm sure that you never wanted to do that in the first place!! So good luck with creating your artwork, and you can do it in one of three ways. Firstly, if you are a graphic or arty type person anyway, I'm sure you would love to do it in Adobe Photoshop or Adobe Illustrator, since you already understand it, and I'm sure you have a creative brain to understand what would make her powerful piece of artwork to represent your podcast.

Secondly, if you are creative, but don't really understand Photoshop or equivalent programmes, there's an easy way to do it, and for free on **Canva.com**. You simply go to their website and type in "podcast artwork", and there are so many templates that you can get inspired by, and adapt, and export in exactly the right format for your podcast. So Canva Is a great way to quickly create artwork, if you haven't much time, or experience in the high-end art programmes.

But of course you're only going to be as good as the templates that Canva give you. So for something that is a bit more unique, you may want to consider the third option, of going on a site like Fiverr or Envato Studio and find a freelancer to create a unique piece of artwork for you. By the way, if you do this, I recommend you to pay the extra to get the layered version of the files, rather than a flat JPEG.

Why? Well, you may find a great designer who comes up with the perfect thing for you, then they suddenly disappear off the website, just as you want an update to it. So if you already have the individual layers, you can pass that onto another designer or update it yourself for future use. Now even though your podcast should have a compelling overall artwork file, consider having a different one each week, slightly different in some way. As long as all of them are attractive enough to pull in new listeners, that's all you want. The existing subscribers will be getting it anyway.

There is a school of thought that a specific title, for that specific week's podcast, is a stronger pull than just the general name of your podcast. So if you have time to create a new graphic for each week, for each episode, it's optional, and you don't have to do it, but many people swear by its effectiveness in marketing.

My Favorite Mur...

No Such Thing As...

Forensic Files

The Dan Bongino...

The Ramsey Show

FEATURED PODCASTS

UPLOADING YOUR PODCASTS TO THE WORLD

In the very early days of podcasts, the producers of each one simply had an MP3 link on their website, and so would use their main website as the place to distribute the podcast and the listeners would simply download the MP3 and then play it on their own device there.

Things are much easier now, and the whole world is much better connected, thanks a lot to the old iTunes, effectively now called Apple Podcasts. These days, more than half of all podcasts are searched for and streamed from Apple podcasts, so do you simply upload your podcast files to Apple? No.

Apple Podcasts is just a directory and a listening app. Many other directories and listening apps exist. Listeners can find you at these places, they can subscribe to your show there, and listen to you there for your podcasts. But, actually they are accessing your podcast from your chosen host.

So, keeping it simple, here's how it works.

1. **You need to choose a podcast host.**

2. **They assign you a special URL, called an RSS feed link.**

3. **You upload your podcast to your podcast host.**

4. **Your host then publishes that episode to your RSS feed**

5. **Your host publishes it, too, to your podcast hosting website.**

Then Apple Podcasts – what used to be known as iTunes, detects the new episode on your RSS feed and if it OK's the information on the form and the graphic you've uploaded, it makes your podcast available to your subscribers.

You can also embed a player on your own website and people can access it there, so that's like the gool ol' days as well!

If all this sounds confusing, let's go things again from a different angle; it's important you understand how it works and choose the best podcast host according to your needs.

First of all, podcast directories like Apple Podcasts, are really listings for your podcast, and they help people find your podcast online. In most cases, they don't host or distribute your podcast. That's all up to your podcast host.

They just provide a centralized place for podcast listeners to learn about podcasts in general. In a way, podcast directories are similar to how we used phone directories.

If you want to podcast about video games, you open up the Apple Podcast directory and you search through till you find "video games" and then you find the top video game podcasts. Getting listed in the top directories is a critical part of your podcast marketing strategy, because a majority of new listeners, when your podcast is new, are going to find your podcast through these directories.

Once someone's subscribed to your show, they connect directly to your podcast via your RSS feed link that connects them to the audio file you uploaded to your host company, and they'll start getting all of your episodes downloaded automatically. It's critical that you get into the top directories, since that's how most people will find your podcast. The top three podcast directories are Apple Podcast, Spotify and Google Podcasts.

Now, if you don't have an Apple account, you need to create one at Podcasts Connect. Once logged into Podcasts Connect, you'll then be asked for your RSS feed address. The important thing is whether it validates it or not. Why might your podcast be rejected?

Well, there are a few settings that you must have in place before you submit your podcast. Make sure you've filled in every one of the following:

Title: The actual name of your podcast
Description: A short summary of your show, focussing on why people should listen, usually 140 characters max.

Category: Most hosts allow up to 3 categories in which you can appear – When you create your own podcast series and submit it to be listed in Apple Podcasts, you need to pick at least 1 podcast category for it to be listed under. There are plenty to choose from. Any listeners browsing these categories for new shows will do so by interest. So, if your fishing podcast is listed under cookery, you're unlikely to get in front of your target audience and attract new listeners. Saying that, the majority of podcast listeners find their favourite shows through word-of-mouth recommendations, or by hearing about them on other podcasts.

Listeners who **do** browse apps like Apple Podcasts will tend to primarily do so using the search function.

So **choosing a good podcast name** and writing good and clear episode titles is far more important than the categories you're actually listed in.

Apple are also becoming increasingly strict on the way their store appears to users. So if your show is listed in a category that's completely irrelevant to its content, you run the risk of being removed from the entire directory.

You can pick up to 3 of these podcast categories in total to match your show topic. This isn't done via Apple, but inside your media host.

As we went through in the "Choosing a niche" section, there are 19 overall categories, and 15 of these are broken into subcategories.

Let's talk Spotify.   This originally of course was set up to broadcast music,
but it's quickly become a really big player in podcasting and the second most popular and important podcast directory.

They open the door to a lot of people who weren't already listening to a lot of podcasts. Only a quarter of people listen to podcasts on a regular basis, but almost everyone listens to music. So it's an opportunity for you to get in front of people who may not be listening to podcasts. Yet getting into Spotify is a great way to expand your podcasts reach.

We need to make sure we have all those things set up. So it's very similar to what we did for Apple Podcasts. You have to have a live episode completed, a title, description, artwork, all of that.
So if you just submitted to Apple Podcast, you're ready for Spotify.

Go to **podcasters.spotify.com** If you host your podcast with one of their aggregator partners, and all the main ones are listed, it's easy to submit your podcast to Spotify! Since Spotify doesn't do a human review of each podcast, you mostly can get approved and listed in about a minute.

Google Podcasts is another podcast directory that can really expand your podcast reach, and Google Podcasts gets you in front of billions of Android users.

Episodes might just end up showing up in Google search results anyway as the 'bots may find your links on your website. Google Podcast's mission is to double the amount of podcast listeners in the world over the next couple of years. So you absolutely want to get your podcast listed in Google Podcasts, but it doesn't have the standard submission process. It's not the same as what we just did for Spotify, for Apple podcasts. Instead, you make sure that you have a podcast website, that it's compatible with Google podcasts and they will add you automatically within a week. If you get your podcasts into Apple, Google and Spotify, you're pretty much done. You're in front of like ninety percent of all podcast listeners, but there's a lot of other directories as well, like Stitcher, Tune-In Radio, I heart radio and so on. There are always new ones popping up.

MARKETING YOUR PODCAST

When you start creating podcasts, even if it's got a very snappy and memorable and relevant title, and superb production values, you want to help listeners find it. You can't finish recording, submit your RSS to the directories and put your feet on the desk, basking in the knowledge of a job well done.

For some things in life, you can subscribe to the mantra of "build it, and they will come". Unfortunately, unless you're very well-known and have got a good press officer, this won't happen. But no problem, just follow these simple tips plus those in the next section, and the magic will happen. If your podcast finds its target audience and you provide a regular diet of what they want, that audience will grow, and grow!

First of all, let's talk ID3 tags. When you create a new podcast episode, the meta information – such as the title of your episode, artist/author, your website URL and any episode-specific artwork – are attached to each episode's media file in what's called an ID3 format.

All that information helps ensure that a listener knows what your episode is about and enables it to display correctly in a portable media player or software-based audio player. You may have a wonderfully stunning piece of artwork, but these tags are so important as well to grab in new listeners.

If a media file is somehow separated from the app that downloaded it, these tags are the only information elements left to let the listener know what they are listening to. When you start to create a podcast, you need to fill in all this information on the forms that you upload, but quite often that information will be the same for every episode, so you may want to investigate a free tagging program such as EasyTag, or Blubrry Powerpress combined with Blubrry hosting, so that this ID3 tagging can be set up automatically.

This means the tags will be written to your MP3 files based on the data you've already entered into PowerPress settings and in the blog post associated with your podcast episode. This streamlines the production process and makes it less likely that your show will get separated from the all-important tagging data.

So how are you actually going to launch your new podcast? Are you going to have a big marketing promotion? Well you could throw money at it of course, but that probably isn't wise. It all depends on the type of Contacts you have already. Maybe you already have YouTube channel , a good presence on social media, and a good network of friends and colleagues, and so you could have a kind of launch like a feature film, or a big TV show with promotions on YouTube, various teases coming out on your social media channels, and a countdown on your website.

But maybe you are not that kind of person, and your podcast would not suit that kind of snazzy launch. So you could be looking for a "soft launch", and this is a marketing term for just quietly starting your venture, without much fuss, and getting feedback from people who find you or you invite to experience it. From this feedback, you tweak it, and then you may wish to do an advertising or marketing push later on when you are absolutely sure it's ready.

Maybe the soft launch would be more suitable if you're a little bit nervous, but it really is incredible how it sharpens the mind, when you actually have a launch date in your diary, and you promoting this date to the world.

Somehow things get done quicker, you're less likely to procrastinate, and somehow the first podcast gets made, and it can be a tremendous success, made with the adrenaline that knowing the launch date was coming up pumping in your veins.

So it's up to you what kind of launch you do, but just be proud about it, don't worry that you may be thinking you are stepping on the toes of other podcasts, or that you are emulating their ideas, or formats, you will soon grow your own identity anyway, and get your own fans; and there have been many occasions, where a clone, or breakaway podcast from an original as actually turned out to be much more successful than the original.

But what do we mean by "success" here? It depends what kind of podcast you are making, and it's a shame in a way that podcasts are sometimes compared to YouTube videos, and if your listening figures for a podcast aren't in their millions like the top YouTube videos are, you feel a failure.

Well, let's put this another way round. Let's say you were giving a talk in person. Physically standing up in the Town Hall down the road from you. You invited local people to listen to you. It doesn't matter what the subject is. If 50 people turned up, or maybe 100, would that be a success for you? All those individuals would have made the effort to physically come along sit themselves down and listen to your talk. And I think for a niche subject, many people would say that is a success. So if your podcast gets 100 listens, you must think of that as a success, it's not like people are listening to a radio show in the background, they would be listening to your every word, as people do when they consume podcasts. Listeners to podcasts are there for a reason. They are actively engaged with the subject you are talking about, they are passionate, and want to listen to what you and your guests have to say.

So forget about the numbers. It's more about the quality of the listener, and that is a measure of success. Every download is a real person, who wanted to engage with you, and hear what you had to say. Just think of that. You should be proud of communicating like that.

Now of course, if you are running not a hobby niche podcast, but a corporate or organisation or podcast, numbers probably DO matter for you here, because you need to report to your bosses about how successful it is. And here, numbers matter.
It also matters when you're trying to monetise your podcast, as you'll need to show the figures to your potential advertisers and sponsors.   If you're in this situation, you will no doubt be listening carefully to the section I have next on how to boost your listeners further,

with many different ideas to get more people to subscribe to you.

So how do you first get started with marketing of a brand-new podcast?
The first thing you can do, and it may seem obvious, although many people forget about it, is to involve their family and their direct friends. Even if they are not actually interested in the subject matter, they'd be interested to see what you're doing, and would be pleased I'm sure, to give you feedback as to the format, the structure, and anything else, which may give you some useful insight to improve it. This approach works particularly well with a soft launch, so you can make any changes for the big official launch, once you have ironed out any initial issues.

You need to find groups of people who would be interested in your podcast, so you need to tell them about it via social media, particularly niche Facebook groups and other social media channels, where you can plant the seed that your podcast is coming along. Rather than just post straight adverts, get permission from the admin in that Facebook group, and get involved with the people in the groups, add value and offer your help and expertise before you even mention the podcast that you are involved with is being launched soon.

When you are an active member of a Facebook group with the same subject as your podcast, you may like to consider uploading regular excerpts, not a link to the whole thing, but just maybe a clip of an interview, that you may think will help some other people. The word "help" is so important here, you need to persuade people that they will benefit from listening to your full podcast. So, it's a bit like creating a promotion for the radio, so you select a clip that will intrigue people to listen to the full programme.

A great way to launch your podcast is to discover questions people are asking about the subject matter your podcast will be dealing with on sites like Quora and Reddit. You may find all sorts of relevant questions that are recent, that you could answer from the top of your head, and you can post the answer to that question in full. Do not, however, simply say "I know the answer to this, listen to my podcast!" That won't work at all. You need to answer the question that you have found on Quora and Reddit and say "for more insights into this topic, please listen to my podcast!" You've got to actually help people, or else you will get people on these forums pretty angry if it's obvious you are just trying to plug your podcast.

The other thing to do is to contact relevant blogs using a similar sort of tactic, or find an established blog that covers the niche that your podcast will be covering. The ideal situation would be to find the blog owner who was interested in partnering with you, and maybe would even like her regular interview slot on your podcast or be offered a job in charge of a certain spot or feature. This has been very successful for many podcast owners, because quite often blog owners are text-based people, who may not have ever thought about creating audio or video content on what they are writing about. So it's a way for another aspect of their work to be shown to the public. So basically, you would help each other, it's a kind of cross promotion.

You may also find YouTube channels covering your subject, and if you can contact the channel owner, a similar relationship can be sought there, and at the very least, you can comment under videos, and find visitors there, who may be interested in your podcast.

But of course, I haven't yet mentioned straight advertising. Maybe you would want to consider Google Ads, or advertising on YouTube, or Facebook targeting people who are interested in your subject matter, but did you know there are organisations set up who do nothing but advertise podcasts?

Sites like **Overcast.fm**, run by Marco Arment, offer dedicated sophisticated podcast advertising services. They help you grow your podcast's audience by reaching passionate podcast listeners on their own terms, natively, right in their podcast app.

Your ads would appear below the controls on the Now Playing screen and in the Add Podcast directory, reaching potential new listeners as they search for new podcasts. Tapping brings up a user interface with all of your episodes, inviting listeners to subscribe with a single tap.

You can see the availability looking down the categories of the podcasts on their site, and some of them sell out pretty quickly, so you may need to book in advance, if you are looking for a campaign for the launch of your particular podcast.

You may need to know that adverts for shows primarily about personal investing, real estate, debt management, or similar topics are permitted only in the Business category.

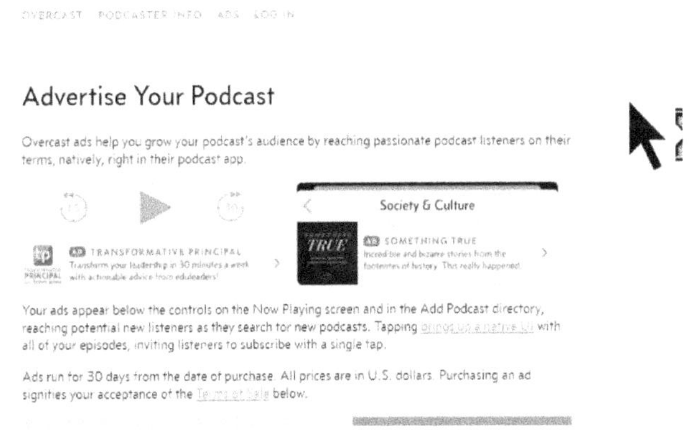

Overcast shares three metrics with you if you buy a package with them; views, taps and subscriptions.

Views: How many times the ad has been displayed to a user in the Overcast app.

Taps: How many times a user has tapped the ad in the app to bring up your podcast's description and episode listing.

Subscriptions: How many users have subscribed to the podcast after tapping the ad. This counts the total number of people who ever subscribed, not the current number who remain subscribed.

Of course, some subscriber loss over time is normal. That's why marketing isn't just something you do at the beginning of a podcast, but is a continual effort to make sure that you entice people to stay with you, and not get enticed by a rival podcast!

And you can log into your Overcast account at any time to view ongoing performance metrics of all current and past ads.

The interesting thing about Overcast is that their prices automatically adjust with demand. After each ad is sold, the price increases for its category.

If a category's available slots do not sell for at least two days, the price will reduce daily until one sells. If a category is usually sold out, its total number of ad slots will occasionally be increased. Overcast are unique in the service that they offer, and the way that they do it, and you don't need to explain what a podcast is, or where to find it, since the adverts will only be going to people who already understand all that.

Of course, the problem is that there are probably more people who don't understand what a podcast is who could very well enjoy your offering. So that's where you might want to consider taking targeted adverts in Facebook, or YouTube.

It can be a pretty daunting thing to start a podcast and then an even more daunting task to market it, but don't worry, as long as the quality is high and so is the enthusiasm of the people behind the podcast, it should gain traction, and there are always lots of other podcast people out there well willing to share their experience with you. So I suggest you join a Facebook group about pod casting, the Buzzsprout one is particularly active community, and Buzzsprout is an excellent company as well who will help you with a whole host of services that you maybe haven't sorted out yet.

Finally, in this section, how can you measure your success? How can you track your reviews and rankings in the niche you are covering? There are many ways to do it, but I would sign up to **podkite.com**, which is a one stop shop to get a good overview of how well your podcast is doing in the world, with all your podcast's chart rankings and reviews in one place. You'll get data from all of the major podcast players and you can get a basic access and information for free; what's not to like?

BOOSTING YOUR LISTENERS FURTHER

I hope I have managed to give you a good steer towards the best way to create record and edit your podcasts, and maybe you're a technical type of person so even those parts of the whole process haven't scared you too much, but in a way that's the easy part, because even if you have the best podcast in the world, if no one hears it, then it's all a bit of a waste, isn't it?

How will anyone actually find you or even know that your podcast exists?
Let's give you some extra tips and tricks to get you some traction, to boost your regular subscribers so that more and more people are listening to your thoughts and your interviews as every podcast comes out. Some of the things I'll say won't be relevant to you, and that's fine, because every podcast is different, and that's the joy of the whole genre.

First, think about your existing fans. I assume you have and existing loyal audience, but it's very small, maybe just the immediate friends and contacts of the people who have helped you put the first podcast together, or if it's an industry podcast, the people who listen are just the main clients of the company you work for and some of the staff.

The first thing to remember is to not to throw the baby out with the bath water. Just keep in mind that the best ambassadors for your podcast are the people who do listen to it, and they aren't just listening to it because it's a favour for you are they? Let's hope there's something in it that they really enjoy, so don't forget your existing audience and you can always persuade them to spread the word for you. So make it easy for them eh?

Reviews are always useful to get but be a bit more specific when asking for reviews in the podcast. You don't want people just to sycophantically say how wonderful you are, but to actually give you some concrete feedback on the specific content that they heard and that they enjoyed or that they found was useful for them. Don't go all heavy and say "Hey, you're getting this for free, you can do something for me in return" or anything!

Make a point of talking about some of the reviews of last week's programme on that week's show. This makes the listeners feel good and warm inside, and they feel a valued part of your podcast family. They will then do their best to advertise to their friends and family.

When you get some good reviews, consider putting them on Twitter, but not as a way to brag, but a way of thanking the person who has given you the review. Don't forget you can find your reviews easily through a whole load of different services. There's **Podkite** as already mentioned but also **Podrover, Chartable, My Podcast Reviews** and many more.

You might also want to tweet a short extract from that week's podcast, made more attractive as an **Audiogram**. Go to **Headliner.app** and they'll show you how you can easily combine a clip from your podcast with some graphics and photos, and an "audiogram" takes up much less space than a traditional video.

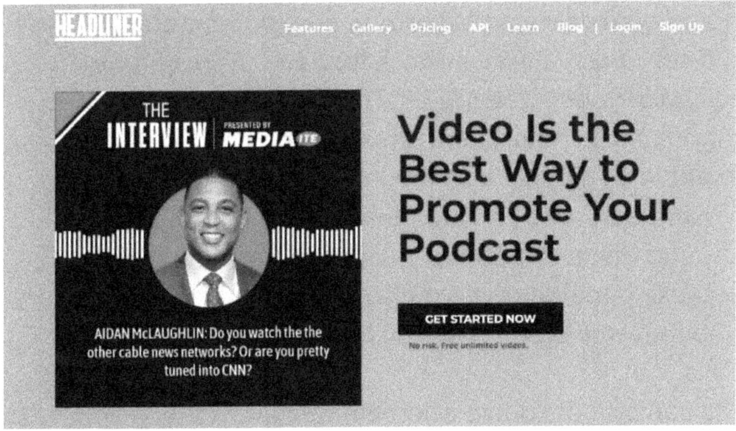

You can also have subtitles as well, as most people browse social media with the sound turned off, so Headliner's app is pretty good for this and the audiogram wizard is very easy to use. Once the Audiogram has been made for you, then simply post it to social media and don't forget to include a link to your podcast website.

Most of the WordPress themes and podcast platforms give an option to include sharing buttons, so your friends can be persuaded to click that button and generate a tweet for example, or an email to give their friends a link to listen to your podcast. You can reinforce this in the actual podcast itself, without going over the top, but by asking your existing listeners to share the podcast links with their friends or anyone else they think might enjoy it. So many people forget to do this, but it's a pretty obvious thing to do. Don't be afraid, you've got a great podcast, just ask your existing listeners to share the word.

There are various social sharing plugins you can use if you are on a WordPress platform so suss out the best of those and see which ones can work for you. Also, you can persuade your listeners to talk about your podcast on various social media platforms, so don't forget to ask them to put in a suitable hash tag, so you can track it. You may of course want to remind them to sign up to your email list, and that's something you should regularly say, because hopefully every episode you'll have new listeners who may not even know you had an email list.

You can also of course ask them to leave a rating and write a review in the app they are listening to your podcast in, such as Apple Podcasts, or there are sites like **Podchaser** which are useful for getting boosts of listenership when people find good reviews. If you haven't even heard of Podchaser, you really need to spend some time looking round there, because you'll find out an awful lot about other podcasts out there, some of which might have very similar niche's to you. And you can see the kinds of things people are saying about similar types of podcast.

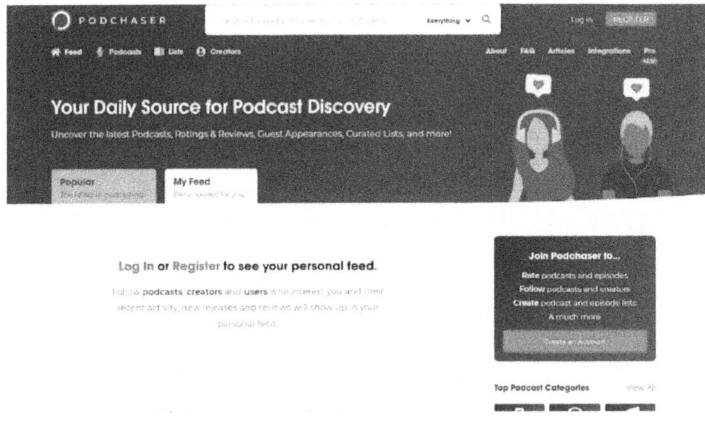

There's also **podchaserpro**, which is a paid version and gives a load of demographics and statistics and contact information for people who really want to go into it to a professional level. If your podcast isn't publicly available, for example if it's a intercompany podcast , or something just for a closed group, it won't be on podchaser, but if you want to submit a podcast there, you just fill in your RSS feed and a bit more information and you could find it very useful to be on there to help your promotional work.

Next, what about netting in people who are new to the actual world of pod casting? I assume you would have a website with various bits of information about your podcast, and that's where an awful lot of newbies end up, along with a lot of confusing little buttons and people are not quite sure what to do. I know, incredible isn't it? But remember it was like that when websites first started, and people were not quite sure what to do with all these funny link buttons and blue underlined bits of text, remember all that?

If someone has organically found you from doing a web search, and are on your website, and have no idea what a podcast actually is – remember not everyone is like us - the least you could do is to give them a bit of information about what a podcast is, and how to actually listen to your own podcasts.

You should have a nice clear list with bold graphics of all of your episodes, and with buttons on there to link to the main platforms and these should be at least Spotify, Apple podcasts, Stitcher , Google podcasts , TuneIn, and iHeartRadio. Now people like us in the game know what those symbols are anyway, but newbies won't know and won't have a clue. So make sure on your website that over there icons for the various platforms, there comes up a tooltip to tell them what it is.
You might even want to have an embedded Vimeo or YouTube video explaining more about how to subscribe to a platform and how to listen to your podcasts on various devices that they're on and how Bluetooth works for connection to many modern car stereos.

Keep it simple; think like a complete newcomer – don't confuse people!

If the thought of having to create a new website too much of a headache for you, especially having to find a web designer, or even an online tool that is podcast friendly, I really recommend that you go to **radiopublic.com** .
They've done a deal with web provider WIX and SquareSpace and can create a superb, professional custom web site for you with all your podcast needs satisfied.
Their sites are designed with custom features for podcasts, like organizing seasons and limited run series, and it

automatically updates when you publish new episodes. You can highlight a trailer and starter episodes and it works with most podcast hosting providers.
There's integration with Google Analytics and you can understand which episodes perform better than others.

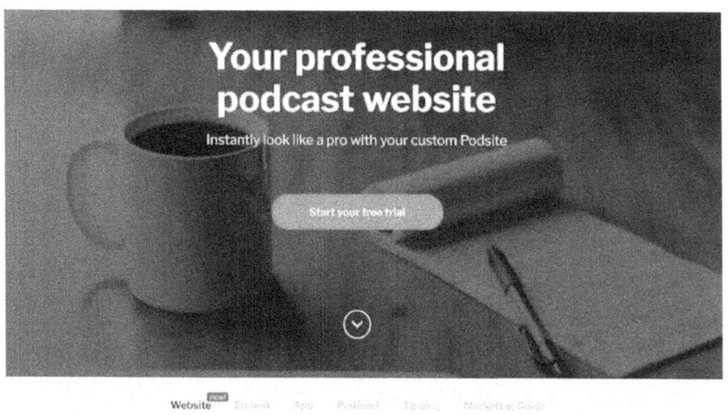

A bonus is that you get paid – not much, but things add up - every time your podcast is heard on your RadioPublic so-called "Podsite". You can even earn more money directly from your fans as it asks them to tip you!
Go to https://podcasters.radiopublic.com/website to find out more.

You should make sure that the homepage for your website is extremely user friendly to new visitors. Your regular visitors will know where to click, but new visitors won't. Why not make a little welcoming video, mentioning some of the topics of your podcasts so far!

By the way, if you are making a promo, for social media or on YouTube, don't waste time by listing all the various directory's that your podcast is available on. Just make sure the name of the podcast is clear and people will find it for themselves. That's why most broadcasters who create podcasts as well as radio programmes don't bother listing the full set of directories that they are listed in, but simply say on their promos *"find us where you get your podcast from."*

Just because all of us are immersed in the world of the podcast, doesn't mean to say that potential new listeners are too, and that's something to keep in mind all the time. People who are experienced in listening to podcasts will have their own favourite directory, such as BBC Sounds, Apple podcast, Spotify, and so on, and they won't even bother to use a normal search engine to start looking for podcasts.

But you do need to remember that many people are just interested in a subject and are not quite sure how they are going to find something else about it. So, when they Google a subject matter, even an extremely unusual niche, they may be quite happy with finding text, maybe a YouTube video, but if there's a podcast as well that's amazing, and you could draw them into this world of intimate audio enlightenment!

So don't forget your master website, that every podcast should have, and you need to regularly make sure it is updated, and you are using search engine optimization, as much as you can, and if there is a budget, maybe you need to outsource this to someone who knows what they're doing, because it can be a full time job in itself! If you are looking for a SEO expert, really check them out, because there are many charlatans out there who simply don't know what they're doing or will charge you a lot of money for no big gain.

There are various SEO plugins for websites you might be interested in, for example for WordPress , Yoast SEO is a great little plug in which has a free version and a professional version for about $100.

If you don't know the basics of search engine optimization, just keep in mind that search engines like Google are forever trawling websites and making sure that when people put in a phrase or word, they will come up with the most relevant websites for you in the search results. You need to try to get your website on the first page of Google results, because very few people go further than that. That's true, isn't it? When was the last time you actually went further than Page 1 on a search result?   So the Google search engine will look at all the text on your website, and hopefully it will be updated regularly, telling the robots that the website is alive and active, and you need to put keywords in there.

These keywords need to be related to the subject in hand. The whole thing is pretty complicated, but if you want to get a very basic list of keywords, you can use the Google AdWords keyword planner and it's free. You just need to load up the tool and use the "search for new keywords" tool.

 If your podcast is about Forex trading, for example you would put this in and ask for all the keywords to do with this subject along with data with how often people have put this into the search engine recently. It's really useful, and somehow you've got to create text on your site which includes these keywords, and the order of words, to show that you are tackling that subject and can offer answers to the questions that people are asking in the search engine. You can look for the number of searches of a particular phrase or couple of words every month, so that shows you how many times people are asking questions or looking up information about it.

This could also give you ideas for future podcast topics. Your pictures are also trawled by search engines so ensure that every picture has an ALT tag and a tool tip that shows up when a mouse goes over it. These things are easy to add in a website creation program, but so many people forget to put them in. You usually right click the photo on your website creation page and then you can type in the ALT tags and so on. You would put these tags on photographs of yourself and your guests, and also of any equipment, or gadgets that you are reviewing on your podcast, as people may search for these, and simply find your site because you have put the tag on the photograph.

As well as including keywords and ALT tags that have been correctly chosen, and sprinkled throughout your main website, a good way to attract people, who are searching via the normal search engines, like Google, is to give great names to your episodes.

Don't just have a name for the whole of your podcast series, and then just number each episode. Each episode should really relate to a certain issue or topic. And ideally, it should answer a question. So many searches on Google, relate to questions. So for each episode, try and think of making the title a question, where the contents of the podcast solved that particular issue, and answer the question. It doesn't have to have a question mark at the end, because search engines are intelligent enough to work it out, so for example, if it is a gardening podcast, instead of just calling it "Garden Ponds" - Work out what the main topic of conversation with you and your experts is going to be, and you may want to retitle it" dealing with garden pond weeds" or whatever.

Unless you have a really well-known interviewee on your podcast, don't title the podcast with their name in the title. For example, if you state on your website for a cycling podcast "Episode 68 – We talk to Harry Banana about replacing brake cables", Google will not find much to harvest.

Which potential listener is going to type into Google "Episode 68" or "Harry Banana"?

So, call the episode as a big, bold title "How to replace a road bike brake cable" with your guest's name in the description under the title. People generally search for solutions to issues or problems, so make it very clear what you are offering.

Forget putting the episode number down, most of the platforms will add it anyway, but it doesn't really matter. Also if you don't number the episodes on the podcast's website, it gives you the flexibility to move things around, or even delete some that weren't very popular, or weren't technically good and you're a bit ashamed of them!

Although I recommend you don't put the episode number, I would put the date somewhere, simply because people might be looking for really up to date information, and they don't want to waste their time listening to an old podcast where the advice has been superseded.

Something else you could do for potential new listeners who find you first on your website, is to have a really decent search facility on your site, so if they are looking for a particular topic that you have already covered, and maybe you have been producing podcasts for a while, they will be able to find that.

Don't put a tiny little search box at the top and assume they know what to do with it, you need to make it quite big and bold and explain that they can put something in there and if the subject has been covered it will show up the episodes. Your web designer should be able to put something like this in for you, but make sure that you don't disappoint people if nothing shows up make sure there is a message that actually says in a friendly manner " Sorry - nothing for that yet, why not contact us and we may do a podcast about this subject!" Then link to an email so you get their message.

If you don't want to go to the trouble of having a sophisticated search system, at least have a very good clear list of your podcast in order first of all of when they were made, and then have a very clear tab where you've got the same podcast but in order of subjects covered there, but of course all this will depend on what your niche is.

Something else on your promotion and marketing list, is to tackle Spotify if you haven't done already. Don't ignore them thinking that they only do music stuff. Of course Spotify was originally set up to be basically an online radio station, with endless music satisfying fans of particular genres, and Spotify intelligently works out that if you like one song you're like another. It's trying to do that with podcasts as well. And that's why the Spotify "dashboard for podcasts" is important to understand, and you put the settings you wish there for maximum effect. You start by logging in and clicking "Claim your podcast" By the way, if Spotify subscribers are not paying for it, they are going to hear commercials, and there's nothing you can do about that. So, there may be an unfortunate situation, where in between your podcasts, your listeners will hear adverts to a rival organisation to one that is sponsoring your podcast, but let's hope that's rare!

The other portal that you need to get on is Google Podcasts. However once you get established, Google may find you! Google trawls the podcasts around the world, and if it likes what it hears, and yes their robots do have ears apparently, you'll be joined to that club. So if your podcast isn't featured on Google podcasts you can actually go to an interface. It's called Google Podcast Manager. **podcastsmanager.google.com**

You can claim your podcast and ensure it's available to millions of podcast listeners across Google Search, Google Assistant, the Google Podcasts app and more.

Now, on the manager, not only can you see if your podcast is listed, but if you are in the Google club, and you are on their directory, they offer pretty cool analytics. For example, you could look up an episode, and not only see how many people have listened to the episode, but when they drop off. So if you see a lot of people losing interest at say, 21 minutes, and you know that's when a certain feature started, you'll know somehow that wasn't popular with those people who decided not to listen anymore. You can understand new listening habits as well, by seeing how your audience listens across devices like smart speakers, smartphones and desktops—and understand how your content is discovered on Google Search.

It's all very clever stuff, and you can't ignore the might of Google can you? You start off by clicking the "start now" button, and then you simply paste in your podcasts RSS feed code. You can make sure that all the information is correct there for your podcast, and then they will send you an email link to verify your ownership. Once that's done you're in, and the fun can begin.

Another huge organisation you can't ignore, is of course Amazon. Now if you have submitted to directory's like Stitcher, or TuneIn, there's a pretty good chance that Amazon would already have you on their directory already. But you need to check this, because things change all the time in the fast moving world of podcast businesses! Amazon is important, because all those people out there who are too lazy to type in the name of your podcast will be asking Alexa to find your podcast and to play a certain episode.

But remember that with smart speakers are not actually that smart when it comes to understanding unusual words, or titles or podcasts that could be spelt or pronounced in different ways. If you haven't yet launched your podcast yet, and you are still considering various titles, maybe you'd like to think of a title which can be easily worked out by a smart speaker.

It needs also to be a fairly short title, because as you know, smart speakers repeat the title that you've asked for, so you don't want to annoy the potential listener every time having to listen to your advertising line that you've included in the title!

Another way you can seek out new listeners for your podcast, is to join clubs that they are members of, then you contribute, and get known there. There are endless Facebook groups on many subjects, that you could try to be a member of various online communities, that may cover exactly the same kind of niche that you want to cover on your podcast. Be sure to offer to the community some tips and hints and contributions in return for you gently mentioning that you have a podcast, and be sure you are not stepping on the toes of the organisers of the online group, who may have a podcast of their own!

A good way of introducing yourself with say, of Facebook group, is to say that you a producer of a podcast dealing with the subject of the Facebook group, and you would appreciate if anyone has any particular hot topics that you could assist them with. With posts on social media in general, you do really need to ask questions of people, and usually people will reply. It's fine to mention podcasts but why not positively mention even some of your rivals of podcasts also covering the niche?

 You will be much better regarded in the various communities, if you aren't just bragging about how good your own podcast is. In fact, you might even want to investigate contacting another podcast where your areas overlap, but each of you have a different area of expertise. And you would have a joint episode or more, where you appear on their podcast and they appear on yours. Just think outside the box, and be creative!

Once you're established a little bit, you may like to try your hand at getting a free promotion from Apple itself. You fill in a form and tell them how great you are, and you never know you may take enough boxes and impress them enough to get promoted by Apple podcasts.   Apple Podcasts editors routinely feature compelling podcasts that consistently post new episodes to help users find new favourites. Although promotion isn't guaranteed and is solely at the discretion of Apple, include strong versions of the following elements in your podcast to give your show a far better chance of being featured:

> **A clear and complete author listing**
> **A robust and accurate description of your podcast and all related episodes**
> **Accurate and relevant metadata, including language, category, and parental advisory**
> **Attractive, original artwork in, ideally, a 3000 x 3000 pixel JPEG or PNG artwork file**

If you're launching a unique podcast or releasing an interesting new season or episode, we want to know about it. Submit an Apple Podcasts Promotion Request with at least two weeks of lead time.

To find more details, Google *"apple podcasts promotion request"*

I've given you loads of ideas here, but often the best ones are the simplest ones. The best ones boil down to engaging with your listeners. As we've mentioned, simply asking them to come up with their own ideas for future episodes, as well as obviously asking them to comment about what they thought about this episode can be so powerful.

In fact, if you have a weekly podcast, and I do encourage you to try and bring one out every week, because that seems to be the optimum time for publishing, make a point of talking about last week's episode, and mentioning some of the comments you have had.

A podcast is essentially like a radio show, and when people hear their comments mentioned on the radio, they do get excited, and very engaged, and that's what you want. Those sorts of people - really engaged listeners, will spread the word for free to your podcast. When you create your intro and outro jingles, which most people have with a piece of music to make it a little more professional and memorable, your so called "calls to action" can be spoken by the voice over in that as well to reinforce the requests to your listeners in case you have forgotten to say them towards the end of the show.

If you have the type of podcast where you need to know exactly who is listening and what the listeners think and want from future episodes you could consider having a survey with some incentives for your listeners to complete for you. You would share a link on your podcast, with an easily memorable and short URL, that you would create in Tinyurl or pretty links, or have a form on your main website.

Ask some sensible questions, not too many, but those that would give you the most valuable insights, and use Survey Sparrow, Zoho Survey, PollDaddy, Survey Monkey or Google Forms and see what you get!

Unless it's a multiple-choice survey, expect to get some people with some home truths that you have to take with a thick skin. Maybe they don't like your co-presenter, maybe they don't like the music at the introduction, or maybe they want you to tackle subjects that you want keen to do? You have to remember how many listeners you have, and how many people have replied to your survey, so you can work out approximately the general feelings, both good and bad towards your podcast.

But you may also consider signing up for a podcast analytics subscription. **Podkite** and **MyPodcastReviews** are pretty reliable for the information they give and cover most of the world and the major platforms. But don't get too hung up on the data, or you'll begin to act like US Network executives looking to cancel a show just because the ratings have dipped a certain percentage.

Podcast listening figures vary a lot over the course of a year, depending on what people are doing in their everyday lives, as well as of course this topic that you have that particular week or the guest you have on, it's a fact of life that some topics and guest interviewees are more popular than others, so don't sweat too much about it!

If you are hunting around to get some income in and looking for a sponsor, don't forget that the sponsor may want to give something that doesn't cost them as much as actual cash. What if your sponsor in return for getting some spot advertising, gave you a voucher for services or goods depending on what the sponsor is? And then of course you have now got some prizes to give away in a competition. Especially if the sponsor and the service and product is relevant to the subject matter of the podcast, this is a win-win situation for all.   Make sure that there is some skill involved, most people like to get the answer of a question right and then they are encouraged to contact you to go in for the competition prize. Remember that podcasts are listened to retrospectively, so don't think that you're only going to have listeners to this week's podcast this week, because all the old episodes are still available. So you don't want to upset people sending in a competition entry, when it closed a long time ago! So just mention on the recording the date when the entries have to be in by.

Something else you may want to consider, is a downloadable PDF, with either a transcript of the whole podcast, or ideally if you have time, you would give a condensed version of that week's podcast, with links and various other bits of extra information that people can download as a PDF for free after the show together with nice pictures or graphics.

The final tip I can give you in this section, and it's one after you have got yourself a bit established, is to go in for a podcast competition. Win yourself an award! I can't really mention any of the contests here, because they change so quickly, but if you do a Google search for podcast competitions, and awards, particularly in the area of podcasts that you specialise in, this is a way of getting some exposure, and helps to spread the word about your show and to expand your reach. Good luck !

MONETIZING YOUR PODCAST

A podcast is really a "radio show". The obvious way to monetize your podcast is to create spot advertising, like you would on a radio station, but the advantage is of course that people listening to your podcast would be extremely targeted, unlike a mainstream radio station. That means you would only feature adverts with products or services of interest to the actual subject you are covering, so this makes the podcast an extremely effective and powerful medium for advertising.

Podcast listeners are actively engaged listeners! Podcasts offer a more intimate form of advertising. This means that podcasts generate excellent brand recall. In fact, according to **podcast-media.co.uk** who specialise in creating advertising campaigns for podcasts, there is 4.4 times Better Brand Recall on podcasts than many other widely-used forms of digital advertising.

With an average listening time of 7 hours per week, UK podcast listeners tune in regularly. Over this time those loyal listeners build up a relationship with the podcast hosts, establishing a high level of trust in the media channel and accordingly the advertising brands. Podcast advertising leads to conversions! 76% of people said that they had followed up on a brand message heard in a podcast and a massive 61% of listeners have brought a product that they heard advertised on a podcast. Podcast listeners pay attention! They don't skip the ads, because they don't want to miss out on the show. In fact 65% of listeners stay tuned for the entire episode.

86% of podcast listeners subscribe to a premium video service such as Netflix, meaning they are difficult to reach through traditional advertising solutions. **podcast-media.co.uk** have estimated that in just the last 2 years, weekly listeners have grown from 5.9 to 11.3 million. And that's just in the little ol' UK! So you can see there is massive potential for generating money for spot advertising.

But before you run off with the idea and start booking your yacht, you need to think of the realities. Until you become an enormously successful podcast, there won't be huge figures of cash involved, and also you don't want to be so greedy to earn advertising money, that the whole flow of your show is ruined because it's full of adverts, which can annoy people, even if they are professionally produced, and targeted at the audience who are listening. A softer way of introducing adverts, is by sponsorship, where the service or product name is mentioned at the beginning and end of the podcast, and you would say something like supported by and then insert the name of the company, with maybe some extra benefits to the sponsor, such as a "live read" script in the show, or you would have some deal to give away some products or service vouchers in the podcast as a competition prize.

It takes a bit of thinking about, and if you want to fully concentrate on producing your podcast, and if you are also doing all the technical side, maybe you would want to outsource this to a company who have experience, and know what they are doing in the market, in return for their expertise.

So why not contact a company like podcast media, who understand the market, know what niche's advertisers are looking for, and what sort of fees to charge. This sort of organisation would also take care of invoicing and doing all the nasty things that I'm sure you won't want to do yourself, and you can just get on with creating your editorially and technically brilliant regular podcasts!

Another way you may like to think about monetising your podcast, is that if you are recording your podcast almost live, as if it was a radio show that began and ended, without much editing in between, is to have a camera or even a couple of cameras recording you and your colleagues putting it together.

Now I know you will need to have quite a bit of technical expertise to do this, but if you have a technical wizard on your team, who could film you, and also insert the video interview with the your guest on Zoom or whatever, you could bring out your podcasts as a video version on YouTube, and monetised these videos in the usual way there. Your personalities would also come across on video as people would be able to see you and understand how your podcast is put together.

Many radio stations do this now, with a webcam so you can see the presenter while they are broadcasting. It's not the most exciting visual experience, but it is intriguing to see the presenter surrounded by equipment and scripts, and it's another option you may like to consider.

So how else can you monetise your podcast? Well, if you really are offering good value with lots of tips, and interviews you could create monthly subscriptions for people, who not only get the free podcast as everyone else does, but bonus episodes, and maybe a membership part of your website, where they would have a password to get other materials and downloadable resource is, that is relevant to your normal free podcast.

You could of course like public broadcasting services around the world, do a sort of "radiothon" where you would ask for donations directly from your listeners, and make it fun with people being sponsored for various things to raise money for the podcast. Just be very careful that people won't feel negatively about you raising money for your podcast production costs, and your back pocket, when there are obviously many charities and poor people out there, who really could do with the money much more!

If you have a podcast niche that often uses equipment, such as fishing, astronomy, cookery and so on, you can do deals with manufacturers or source new gadgets and you can sell them via your podcast by trying them out, reviewing them, and offering a perceived discount to your listeners.

Of course, you would have done a deal with the manufacturer or distributor, to get the gadgets at even better prices, so you would make a profit.

Why not record interviews with the team who designed the gadget or created the service you're featuring? You could ask: What problems did consumers have before this came out? How long did it take to test? Tell us the success storeys behind it so far? Rather than you and your colleagues just guessing about all this, get it from the horse's mouth, and it will be a much more interesting podcast, if you actually have an interview which may lead into a proper sponsorship or partnership deal with the company.

If they are happy with how it goes you may get even more products to review and to maybe give away their products on competitions. Remember the podcast is a bit like the Wild West, you can do virtually whatever you like, as long as it's not obscene or illegal, so you can run ads and do sponsorship deals . It's not like you're following the strict rules of the British Broadcasting Corporation or something like that!

What about creating your own gadgets and products, from feedback you have got from your own listeners? You certainly could create and sell apps that meet the needs of your listeners. An awful lot of knew apps have come about by people passionate about a certain niche, realising that something was missing, and would be very useful in their life if they had something. So think about that, and you could make a good income from creating an app via your podcast.

How about re purposing the content in your podcast? You might want to consider creating an ebook, or even the audio edited together into audio book content, and upload it to audible via the ACX.com platform.

When podcasts are really popular, the boot can be on the other foot when it comes to guests. Instead of pleading with experts to come on your podcast for free, or even to pay their expenses, or fees, guests can often pay podcast producers to be on their show. This is especially true when they have something to sell, like a new book. So good luck with monetizing your podcasts!

PODCASTS FOR BUSINESS

If you're old enough to remember when the internet first came along, you'll also remember there were many companies and organizations who thought it was just "a fad", "a gimmick" and thought, "we don't really need a website, do we?" Well, of course, these days everybody needs a website, even small traders often need one as well to survive. One day, and it will come soon, every business will realize they should have a podcast of some kind for their clients, or at least to get involved in an existing podcast that they can guest in.

Podcasting is unique in that being audio, you can actually consume them while you're doing other things. You are also much more likely to be drawn into it, and less likely to skip forward or find other things like you do when you are browsing videos on You Tube.

If you have an organisation that still produces a weekly or monthly newsletter or magazine for staff and clients, can you with your hand on your heart, say that it is welcomed and is read from cover to cover? Does your heart sink having to throw away piles of unread staff magazines or client newsletters, and are you also concerned about the cost of design, printing, and the mailing out of these things?

This is where the podcast really scores, because it is a modern means of communication, very quick to make, and above all it is personal. People will be listening to you and your colleagues at your organisation talking about what you are doing what are you planning for the future, and all the news that is concerned with what you do as an organisation. Everybody will have a smartphone, and most modern cars have got a Bluetooth stereo system, so it's easy for staff and clients to listen to your podcast on their way to or from the workplace, and it makes a change from listening to depressing news programmes!

Because you'll be using your podcast to share useful information in conversation form, your audience feels they are benefiting from your broadcasts – because they are!

You'll be continually delivering useful info to your customer base building both brand loyalty and brand awareness. If you want word of mouth to help bring in new customers, podcasting is for you. Why? When you give your customers something free, they are apt to tell their friends. Remember, there are a lot of free info sites online, but most of them are thin on content. This frustrates customers.

You can stand out by sharing fantastic information. The more your customers love your podcasts, the more they'll tell their friends about them. This helps spread the word freely, and, again, positions you as an expert.

The important thing to remember when it comes to business podcasts is that people will not subscribe to it, if they know they are just going to be sold things all the time, you are not putting together advertorials. You are not there just to sell your services.   The point of a company podcast is to gently draw people into your world, to help people know you and to trust you as an expert in your field. Your podcast should attract people who are interested in the sort of thing that your organization does, whether it's a bank or a financial services company, it makes paintbrushes, provides cleaning services, bakes bread, promotes road safety or whatever.   Each podcast should be able to focus on one particular area of the overall niche that would be interesting for the target audience.

Your listeners should simply enjoy your news and opinions and the conversations you are having with your guests, you should wow them with the insights and news that you have researched for the podcast content, so they'll trust you more.   And that will develop a better, stronger bond between your organization and the listeners and that should indirectly improve your sales.

Do not try to be all things to all people. In a large organisation, which have different departments, maybe engineering, sales, HR, production and so on, you may be tempted to create a general radio programme with features about everyday life, or sport, or things that affect people outside of work. That's not going to get you subscribers. The raison d'etre of a podcast is that it can drill it down into very specialised niche subjects.

Now this may seem strange that we are looking for niche subjects, but it is far better to have a group of listeners who are extremely interested in the subject matter, then to have a larger listenership who could either take it or leave it, or prefer listening to general lifestyle or sport on a professional broadcast radio station.

If it going to promote your company or organisation, the subject matter of every podcast must be very focused in what your organisation actually does, and gently promotes its aims but without direct selling. You may think this is going to restrict you terribly, and you will run out of ideas in a few weeks, but I promise you you'll be surprised how many different features you can find. Whether you run a factory creating physical goods, or you have a business selling services, all sorts of different subjects can pop up with a little bit of thinking. If your job at an organisation is to create a series of podcasts, think if you were in the shoes of the target audience, and try and imagine what kinds of things would interest them.

Would it be a profile about the managing director, would it be a look at the future of a certain kind of product that you are currently producing, is it some insight into future products all services, or how your organisation is dealing with the current issue or problem? Try to keep in mind all the different types of listeners you have, but still keep in within your organisation niche; so that, for example, if you are covering a subject that is very technical, one week , the next week would not be so technical in case it puts some people off, and so on.

 It can be hard to keep the pot boiling with a weekly podcast, for a type of business or industry where there's really not much happening in it. . That's where your research comes in. This is where you would need to subscribe to various industry magazines online and get notifications of what is happening. And don't forget it need not be in your own country, but it could be relating to any other country or area of the world, which also is dealing with your service or product. Quite often, other companies and countries learn from each other over techniques and ways of working and new products coming out. We can all learn from each other. This sort of thinking will get your mind to think of lists of subjects.

So once you've done your research and thought of some decent subject matters, then get your diary or wall chart out and make sure you have at least enough strong subjects for the next half dozen or so podcasts. . Of course, there may be a big news story that may push one out of its slot for that week, , and that's fine. That's the advantage of a podcast, in that it is quick to record and edit and there is no delay that you would get with the old design printing and distribution of a physical newsletter or magazine. By the way, if you are in an organisation that isn't fast moving, or hand to mouth, you may want to consider planning half a years' worth of podcasts.

 That way you will get more flexibility and more interest in the podcast. For example, if you were considering 20 podcasts, you would identify 20 interviewees, and instead of spending each podcast with one interviewee, you would have a subject for each week, a topic, and then when you do your interviews, you would ask questions that would fill 20 of the programmes on each topic. That means that in each podcast, each of your experts will have their say on that particular topic. Of course this will only work if news events don't overtake you, but it's worth considering as it makes a useful change sometimes to hear different people speak.

If you're a fan of any talk radio programmes, you'll know that they are often highly structured. And you should take a leaf from the book of broadcasters for your own podcasts. In other words, you should start professionally with some kind of short introduction spoken by another voice ideally, with maybe a short piece of music. Then you would welcome people, as you would to a radio show, and give a little menu of what's on the podcast. each week should have a similar structure, because that way people get used to what's coming up approximately at what time. People like familiarity, and people like to know what's coming up in any programme that they are enjoying on TV, radio, or if it's a podcast.

So maybe each podcast will have a couple of interviews, maybe there would be one interview from inside the organisation, and one from outside. There may be a diary feature in every podcast, or maybe there could be a job section at some point, listing some of the changes and opportunities coming up at various branches. They could be a "did you know" type feature every week, or a handy tip, or safety information of some sort.   You might consider interviews with staff on a particular subject every week, a sort of "we asked you "type feature, in broadcasting these are known as Vox Pops , which is Latin for the voice of the people !

Of course, every podcast of course will be different, but if you can put any kind of structure in it, it will help people to know where they are, and they will feel comfortable listening every week when there is a format that they can relate to. At the end of the podcast, of course you would thank people for listening and you can trail the features to be covered in next week's podcast, and you would invite people to contact you by email usually, or via your website where they can suggest features for future podcasts. You really are playing the part of a radio programme host in a corporate or business podcast, and the whole feel should be professional, to reflect the professionalism of the business.

Now, even though I have stressed the importance of a professional sounding podcast, that's not to say you can't have some fun on it, and make sure that your personality and those of your colleagues come across clearly. So how can you increase the listenership of a business podcast? First of all, you need to make sure that they do come out at a very regular basis. There's no point having a podcast every month, and definitely not every quarter. People need to get into the habit of listening, and usually the weekly podcast is the most successful.

Most people these days still have the weekend as a time when they have time to listen to these things, so many company podcasts are released Friday lunchtime. That's when you would send out a link that would be picked up on people's business email. Then they would be more likely to remember to listen to it on the way home, or over the weekend. You may like to think of some incentives for people to listen to your podcast , but if it's aimed at clients, doing a competition or a special offer gets close to the selling aspect which as I mentioned earlier, is a bit of a turn off. But if your podcast is aimed at staff, why not have a competition where there are prizes for answering questions that are relevant to what you do in your organisation? It's a way of training your staff, as well as rewarding them and having a bit of fun at the same time!

The great thing about audio is that it is very quick to produce. Podcasts can be recorded, edited and uploaded in a hour or two. And of course, you may want to bring out special podcasts in a week where there is a lot of news or activity in your own particular area of business or expertise. It doesn't have to be good news either, it could be a lot of concerning news, over maybe a takeover, or the purchase of your organisation, or rumours of redundancy's. This is where the personal sound of the people's voices involved in the situation is extremely important. Rather than just reading what a managing director is saying for example, hearing their voice on our podcast being interviewed about any proposed changes will come over much more personable, and may help people to understand the situation far more, than just merely reading words in a memo to all staff.

IDEAS FOR BUSINESS PODCASTS
New ideas and technologies.
The history of our brand / product / service.
A maverick interviewed – an unusual view.
Surveys and data analysed.
"Meet the team" interviews.
How to attract bright graduates into our industry.
News of an award we are going for.
Organisation anniversary.

SETTING UP A PODCAST PRODUCTION COMPANY

Podcasts are really big news, and like audiobooks, are growing in popularity enormously. People around the world now realise how wonderfully flexible the audio medium is.

Yes, videos are also powerful and enjoyable, but they are not as flexible as audio content, and you can take an audio podcast with you while you're driving, on a visit to the gym, or on a long walk, to your breaks at work, and you can really get involved with the content.

As I've mentioned, broadcasters around the world have realised how important podcasts are and their ever-increasing demand, and experienced radio producers are now creating podcasts available for download, "programmes" that don't have any of the usual restrictions for content and strict duration parameters that a normal broadcast programme would put on them.

So, doesn't it make sense to create a business that produces podcasts for clients and create an income stream doing this? Your clients would be people who haven't got the time or particularly the technical ability to put podcasts together. If you are a studio owner, or voice over with their own home studio, or maybe someone with broadcast radio feature or news experience, you'd hit the ground running, wouldn't you?

This section is called "setting up a podcast production company", but that sounds rather grand doesn't it, and it could be just yourself as a freelance voice over and narrator, with your own studio now extending your services, offering companies or other individuals who don't know how to produce or haven't got the time to create their own podcast. It could also be that the end client, say an organisation, want the final podcast to sound slick and polished and they want to hire professional voice actors to host the podcasts, rather than use their own staff who may not have the time or the inclination to perform in front of a microphone.

There are various ways of doing this as a Podcast Production company, you might want to act a little bit like a voice over agency, where you would have a variety of ages and ethnicities of professional male and female voices on your books, maybe different accents as well for your clients to choose from, and then when one is chosen, you would simply book the selected voice over to record the script that you would have written for them, or you would ask them to have a Zoom or ideally a Riverside.fm call with an interviewee and give them some questions to ask. Then you'd edit the interview and send the recording to the client for inclusion into their podcast and you'd invoice them. The booked voice artist would then be paid by you.

The problem with this sort of outsourcing is that if you have various random freelancers writing and presenting material that isn't really their niche, then it's just like an actor reading a script, and sometimes for the listeners, the passion for the subject matter seems to be lost, and interviews done this way can seem a bit flat, even though the voice of the interviewer may be wonderful, simply because the hired voice actor interviewer has little knowledge of the subject they're discussing!

This is why, if you are putting together a directory of narrators and voice overs to be used in a company podcast, and you are coordinating them, make sure you find out the interests of your narrators before you post them on your podcast production website. If they have any interests or knowledge on the subject matter of the organisation that you are thinking of putting them forward to, it gives them a much better chance of being accepted and understanding the subject matter that they'll be involved with.

So, if you are setting up a service for companies who want a podcast made, you would really need to involve members of that company in it, as much as you can, to make sure you get feedback at all stages of the production process, to ensure that you are all on the same page. The personality of a company needs to come through, if it is to be useful as a business and communication tool. But if at the organisation, there is no skilled and experienced person to actually put the podcast together, and to actually record and edit and distribute it, then there's nothing wrong with using a company as long as you do your very best to get "under the skin" of your client and understand what they do and what their clients want.

So who would your clients be? There are many organisations, medium and large who bring out regular magazines in a printed format. The same information can appear on their website or as PDFs emailed to their clients, but the information is put together in a form for people to read in a text format with some pictures and graphics. Obviously for the printed company magazine or newsletter, there is no way of knowing who actually reads it, and the expense of printing and distributing a magazine can be very large. And then add to the equation the long time it takes to layout the text, graphics, photographs, and it all has to be checked, then printed then stapled, then sent back and then distributed. If an organisation is a fast moving one, where there is a lot of information happening fast and it needs to be distributed fast, a regular podcast is surely a better medium for doing this. A podcast can be created in hours and be all the more powerful for being topical. Podcasts can be very powerful to market any business and this is what you need to communicate to sell your services.

You need to tie in money making potential of a podcast when you approach potential clients too. Advertising or taking sponsorship with a podcast can be far more effective than with traditional media. Finding niche audiences can be difficult with many types of traditional advertising platforms. Even if you manage to penetrate a niche market through the "click and select" targeting of Facebook or Google Ads, you now need to deliver unique content to that audience. Podcasting allows you to segment your content marketing. You can chop up each episode, pulling content that relates to different niche audiences. This gives organisations the ability to provide different segments of their customers with content that matches their own specific needs.

So, let's talk practicalities. Say you would like to offer a podcast production service to an organisation who need to get information out there regularly to their staff and / or to their clients; and by the way, you could easily make two versions of each, aimed at both audiences; where would you get the content for each podcast from?

You're not an expert on what the organisation does or makes. Well, no problem. As I've mentioned, the existing people in charge of finding all the news articles and features for the in-house magazine or newsletters and the press department who bring out press releases for the organisation, would give you all this information, and you would work with them to decide on topics and subtopics for each podcast episode, and put together a series for them. You'd charge the production and distribution fee.

Now there are still quite a few people who still don't understand what the word "podcast" actually means. Don't assume that everybody does. So, when you sell it to a potential organisation probably via the press office or marketing department, you may have to describe it as a "radio programme", that anybody can hear for free on a variety of different devices. But be careful when you first approach people, they may actually be very tech savvy and be a huge podcast fan, so you don't want to patronise them either!

You would sell the fact that it could feature the voices of people involved in the organisation, and quite often this is a big selling factor as it often boosts people's egos; maybe they're always wanted their own "radio show"!
You would also mention that if you produced podcasts for them, it would save money on a printed magazine, and the production process can move much faster.

In your sales pitches, if you still need any more information to help to persuade your client to take you on as a podcast producer, you need to go on about the power of audio, and how different people taking information in different ways.

You'll know this already if you have studied NLP or Neuro-linguistic programming, that some people are more effective at reaching by text, some by actually touching or using the products you are trying to sell, some simply by looking at photos or charts and graphs, but the auditory side of things is also very powerful, and it's been proven by many psychological studies that hearing the human voice helps the marketing message stick. What's more, the enthusiasm in a voice translates to a longer lasting memory of what the voice is saying.

When you are simply reading text off a screen or page, there is no voice in the head apart from your own. Using audio can help to form a very strong bond between the customers and the marketing message that you're trying to get across to them.

Audio is also very inexpensive to record and edit, compared to print and to video production, and you can also transcribe any audio content into text anyway, so you can engage another group of people. The similar content from the original audio, can be transferred to the company website, an email newsletter, blog, and general social media post, so it's extremely flexible and cost effective. Another advantage of podcast is that listeners can multitask while they are listening, whereas videos need to have full attention.

So have a think about some of the organisations that maybe you know someone in already, who would be interested about you creating a series of podcasts for them. In fact, this could be a full-time job, bringing out a weekly podcast. Staff and clients would be emailed with the details of the content of this week's podcast, and the details of a dedicated website where all the existing episodes could be listened to. We'll have more on the importance of a website later on and what needs to be on it.

Let's say you're an existing narrator, voice artist or audio producer, and so you know about the technical side already. You could offer your services as a presenter and/or producer of a podcast, or at least two record the intro and outro sections, or the intermediate introductions, and then for the rest of it, you would set up record edit and optimise contributions from various people using an internet system. I'm saying this, because I don't want to give the impression that you could only make podcasts for organisations or companies that are in your physical local area.

Yes, it would be nice if you could physically pop in and see people, with your microphone and recorder to get contributions and so on, but that kind of restricts you doesn't it, and a much easier way to do things and with pandemics in mind is safer away, is to do everything online. And that is perfectly possible. It's not as if you have to go in and film anything, it's audio, just audio! It also makes your potential list of clients grow enormously of course, as the whole of the English-speaking world is yours!

The obvious system would be Zoom, or Skype, since most people know how to do this, but if you are in the audio world already, we would recommend that you use a system that uses enhanced audio quality via a browser the Internet. You're only going to use the audio part of a video for their contributions for your podcast.

So make the most of the audio quality. When you're setting up your interviews, you can always do a Zoom call there, which is more friendly, and both of you can see each other, but for the actual recording for your podcast, use an internet-based system. If you are a voice over artist already, or have access to a studio, you may already have a subscription to Source Connect, SessionLink Pro or ipDTL. So why not continue to use these?

If you don't have a subscription already, I suggest that you look into Cleanfeed, Riverside or one of the systems that offer superb quality where you guest is recorded locally – at their end, and you automatically receive the file afterwards – more details are in in the "Recording-Software and Cloud Solutions" section.

VOICE IMPROVEMENT

Now what if you really are desperate to present a podcast, but are worried about the quality of your voice? Is it too high? Too mumbly, or lacking in clarity or authority?

There are many things that you can do to improve the voice, and for many years I have created detailed courses on voice improvement on voiceovermasterclass.com. But here for you, I give you I suppose my "Greatest Hits "of that voice training which I hope will be useful for you. Here are the very basics that every voice actor, podcast presenter and public speaker should do regularly.

First of all, the most important exercise every voice actor should do is to sleep well! Not much of an exercise you may think, but after a heavy day in the recording studio, a decent night's sleep, helps you reset your hard-working vocal folds, and decent sleep, together with keeping your hydration levels really high with pure water, being sensible with alcoholic drinks, eating well, and generally looking after your health will pay enormous dividends to the quality and consistency of your voice.

Secondly, hum! A very easy exercise to do whenever you're alone having a walk, driving a car, or in any spare time, is to hum low down.   Keep to one note for a while, and then slide your humming up and down.   Resonant humming helps you relax as well, which is a bonus, but low resonant humming helps to exercise your larger vocal folds, that are often only used as a sort of human subwoofer in your vocal apparatus.

So, get to exercise all areas of your voice equipment, as well as improving your general resonance, and this will improve the flexibility in creating character voices of all registers from low to high.

Thirdly, you should do daily stretching exercises, to keep enunciation high.   It's best to get a daily routine of a short list of the ones that most benefit you and the age you are and the type of body you have, but here is my personal daily list that takes me 10 minutes in the morning before I get into the voice booth for the first script of the day.

1 – Head turns, not jerking, left to right and up and down.
2- Massage your shoulders to release tensions, or ask a friend to do this from behind. Tensions are the enemy of the resonant and flexible voice.
3- The big yawn exercise is great – just open wide and waggle from left to right, gently. If it turns into a proper yawn, that's fine. The half-yawn is a good base for many a good character voice too, try it!
4 – Lip trills are good too for enunciation, just sound like an old telephone, purse your lips and trill away.
5 – Tongue waggle! Get that tongue wagging and try to achieve the holy grail of describing a perfect circle with the tip of your tongue! I've never met anyone who can do the tongue circle properly!
6 – Finally it's QEQR! The tiny, taut Q sound, the big stretch of the mouth wide for the E, the tiny Q again and then a wide R for the big final!

You don't need to actually say the letters, it's the stretching that's important.

Do these or a more customised set of voice acting exercises every day and it'll repay you enormously.

FINALLY...
Don't take your voice for granted, you need to look after it, especially as it's about to be the star of your new podcast series! If you'd like to find out more information about improving your voice in anyway, or look at our course on confidence if that's an issue for you behind the microphone, please find out more at www.voiceovermasterclass.com.

I hope you have found all this interesting, and you are now fired up and enthusiastic about setting up, recording, editing, and marketing to the world your podcasts. Good luck for the future!

Peter Baker, Author
Written, Spring 2021, UK